The Modern Predicament

Essays and Reviews by George Scialabba

The Modern Predicament

Pressed Wafer | Boston | Massachusetts

Copyright © George Scialabba 2011

ISBN 978-0-9831975-6-0

FIRST EDITION

Pressed Wafer, 9 Columbus Square, Boston, Massachusetts 02116
Printed in the United States

Contents

What Do Moderns Want?

Put simply, the question that animates this book is: What do we really want? To stride off into the sunset or stay home and cuddle? To fulfill the expectations of the people around us or march to our own particular drummer? The fancy term for this is the "dilemma of modernity," and it's also one of the most inescapable and ubiquitous themes of American culture. In the middlebrow fiction of the last few decades, from Philip Roth through Richard Ford and Jonathan Franzen, men struggle to overcome their restlessness and find something heroic, or at least tolerable, about the settled, suburban condition. Women in mass-market literature, meanwhile, have been leaving men behind as they set out in search of fulfillment—or at least superlative pasta and enlightenment—on their own. Classic rock lyrics constantly reiterate the choices: "Should I stay or should I go?"; "We Are Family" or "Ramblin' Man"?—and it was the defiant, heavy-drinking, sexually polymorphous Janis Joplin who left us with the sobering admonition that "freedom's just another word for nothing left to lose."

This dilemma—or ambivalence—runs through my own biography, politics and daily life. On the one hand, my sociable and socialistic impulses run high. I've known, perhaps more than many of my countrymen, the inspiriting strength of solidarity—the emotional bond that unites people working or fighting for a common cause, the joy of marching and chanting "the people united cannot be defeated," or words to that effect. I even get a faint buzz from the good-natured apolitical crowds at street fairs, concerts, or parades. Some of my happiest postcard-style memories involve long afternoons spent outdoors with good people, talking and laughing while the children run underfoot. Family sustains me.

Such intense sociality appears to be hardwired into the human psyche. Outside of the social insects, we are the most socially connected of creatures, usually choosing to live in groups or complex networks of groups and spend most of our time with our conspecifics. According to evolutionary biologists, one of our greatest achievements as a species was to figure out how to live in stable bands of 100 or more—large enough to mount a collective defense against predators and, eventually, against hostile bands of other humans as well. Early humans invented all kinds of techniques, including music and ritual, to promote harmony and keep the group ready to respond, in a coordinated way, to sudden danger or opportunity. In the Paleolithic Era, the stakes were high: If we still fear loneliness and abandonment more than anything, it's because expulsion from the group once meant certain death.

This primordial group-centeredness remains etched into our bodies and brains. Babies need handling and hugs or they fail to thrive; children need stable, reliable adults in their lives. Married people and members of tight-knit religious congregations appear to have a health advantage over single nonbelievers, with, in some studies, fundamentalists doing better than adherents of less rigid theologies. According to social psychologists, moods are "contagious" within human groups, including strangers on a street. Even particular sets of motions, as in dance, can spread by contagion between individuals, thanks to the recently discovered "mirror neurons" that prime us to imitate the actions of our fellow humans in the same moment that we observe them.

But like most of the people I know, and certainly most of those who think of themselves as intellectuals, I am also wary of the coercive power of groups and have been willing at times to risk social isolation by taking unpopular stands. Feminism, for example, was still a target of widespread derision, as well as contempt from many parts of the left, when I first discovered it in the early 1970s, and I know what it's like to live in the only house on the block not draped with flags and yellow ribbons.

I remind myself that majorities have been wrong again and again—about slavery for example, child labor or genital mutilation—while lone individuals or small groups of rebels have been right.

In fact, human survival may depend as much on our capacity for lonely dissent as on our desire to fit in with the majority, or the crowd, and its traditions. One of the most notorious downsides to our avid sociality is groupthink, or the tendency to suppress individual critical judgment in favor of the dominant assumptions or narratives. In his experiments in the 1960s, social psychologist Solomon Asch found that people will alter their stated perception of something completely uncontroversial—like the relative lengths of two lines—in order to conform with what others claim to be observing. This tendency to "get with the program" can be dangerous when it leads to overlooking the possibility of a seemingly unlikely event, like a financial meltdown or terrorist attack by airplane.

If the judgments of the group cannot always be trusted, neither can the group's cherished institutions and traditions, some of which may turn out to have outlived their economic or ecological relevance. Today's dominant religions, for example, are rooted in the experience of semi-nomadic herding peoples who lived 2000–4000 years ago and struggled mightily to maintain their populations—by, among other things, permitting polygamy and discouraging any role other than childbearing for women. Maybe such policies made sense under harsh desert conditions, with high infant mortality and the constant threat of being overwhelmed by more populous or better-armed groups. But in a world where overpopulation, resource depletion, and global warming pose much larger threats to human survival, the pro-natalism enshrined in the ancient religions could be suicidal. Someone has to be willing to point that out—even if a few altars get knocked over in the process.

So where do I stand in the great debate over modernity that is so artfully laid out in the essays that follow? Though I'm one of the polemicists cited, I have to admit that I am perpetually divided. I agree with cultural "conservatives" like Christopher Lasch when they decry the atomization of our society and the destruction of community by the relentless forces of capitalism. At the same time I am almost instinctively drawn to the radicals and dissidents—queer activists, countercultural artists, bitter comedians—who challenge community mores in the name of individual freedom. And even this formulation greatly over-simplifies things, since the lone radicals are usually striving to create alternative communities, while the upholders of "traditional values," like community solidarity, may find themselves cast as dangerous radicals.

Maybe "modernity" isn't the most useful rubric for the dilemma of community versus individualism. Throughout human history and prehistory, most people, most of the time, have probably found themselves scrambling to adjust to circumstances that challenged traditional social relations and ways of doing things—migrations, conquests, technological innovations. They have faced rebellious youths or foreign customs, threats to patriarchy (and perhaps, at some point, in some settings, to matriarchy) and established belief systems. If so, the angst that this book so vividly documents is nothing new. As long as we exist as a species, we'll be debating what constitutes morality and virtue, and we could hardly have a better guide than George Scialabba.

Barbara Ehrenreich is the author of *Blood Rites, Dancing in the Streets, Nickel and Dimed,* and many other books.

The Modern Predicament

Shocks of the New

A specter haunts the late-20th-century American left: the specter of anti-modernism. Jackson Lears, a brilliant young social historian, writes *No Place of Grace: Antimodernism and the Transformation of American Culture* to prove that capitalism has assimilated or trivialized once radical ideals of individual freedom, and that only pre-modern values and loyalties—family, community, religion—can sustain radical protest. Whereupon Morris Dickstein author of *Gates of Eden*, a fine cultural history of the '60s, comes out swinging, accusing Lears of being "captured by a conservative and backward-looking vision . . . the bleak tradition of cultural pessimism." In a series of essays, political theorist Jean Elshtain chides fellow feminists for their "obsession with 'self'" and with "personal development" and for their neglect of traditional values and obligations. Whereupon Barbara Ehrenreich, co-author of the feminist classic *For Her Own Good*, engages Elshtain in a bitter and not very sisterly exchange. Looming over all, enigmatic and aloof, Christopher Lasch hurls thunderbolts of erudite disapproval whenever the contemporary "culture of narcissism" threatens to infiltrate the left.

A key text in this debate is Marshall Berman's *All That Is Solid Melts into Air: The Experience of Modernity*.* Leading his jaded and disheartened late-20th-century readers through the history and literature of the last two centuries, Berman, a political-philosophy professor at CCNY, tries to impart his sense that it all adds up to more than sound and fury and cataclysmic violence. The colossal, often lethal, pains of the modern era have been growing pains, he argues. In any case, we can't go home again; it's too late to stop now; modernity is here to stay.

*Simon & Schuster, 1982.

And we don't really want to go home again, Berman suggests, not even at our most beleaguered. But since even the best sometimes lack all conviction, he amiably, generously offers to share some of his, to help us get our bearings and take heart before going down to the street to grapple with the modern flux.

"What is Enlightenment?" asked Kant at the end of the 18th century. He answered with the first and still perhaps the most famous definition of modernity: "Humankind's emergence from its own minority. . . . And its new motto is *sapere aude*: dare to know." This in essence is also Berman's notion: modernity as maturation, emancipation, critical consciousness, childhood's end. Like adulthood, modernity is inevitable but also precarious, vulnerable to the archaic terrors of a dependent childhood, continually tempted by "transcendent" loyalties rooted in those terrors and that dependence. After childhood, adolescence, with its promise and danger: our present state. Berman's earnest, magnanimous book is an inquiry into how we might survive our culture's troubled and possibly terminal adolescence.

The heart of *All That Is Solid* is a splendidly imaginative reading of Marx as a proto-modernist and of the *Communist Manifesto* as "the first great modernist work of art." In the opening section of the *Manifesto*, Marx describes, with extreme intensity and compression, the rise of capitalism and its destruction of pre-modern forms and traditions. Competition, commodity production, the division of labor, technological innovation, centralization—all relentlessly erode the privacies and privileges of the old world. Economic "rationality" is as pitiless as scientific rationality; economic "superstitions," like self-sufficiency, the intrinsic value of work, and the prestige of the "higher" professions, are no less doomed than theological ones. In Marx's vertiginous prose:

> The bourgeoisie cannot exist without constantly revolutionizing the instruments of production, and thereby the relations of production, and with them the relations of society. . . . Wherever it has got the upper hand, it has put an end to all feudal,

patriarchal, idyllic relations. It has torn asunder the ties that bound man to his "natural superiors," and has left no other nexus between man and man than self-interest and cash payment. . . . In a word, for exploitation veiled by religious and political illusions, it has substituted naked, shameless, direct, brutal exploitation.

All fixed, fast-frozen relations, with their train of ancient and venerable prejudices, are swept away, all new-formed ones become antiquated before they can ossify. All that is solid melts into air, all that is holy is profaned, and man is at last compelled to face with sober sense his real conditions of life and his relations with his kind.

Berman asks: what sort of culture, psychology, and character structure have these changes produced? By way of answer, he adumbrates the modern ideal of individual development: activity, growth, autonomy, self-consciousness, adaptability to incessant change. A new, more mobile personality is needed to survive in a competitive market society. And to excel in such a society requires immense, sometimes overweening energy, imagination, and ambition—qualities we now call "Faustian."

Goethe's Faust, according to Berman, is one of the exemplars of modern dynamism: a "consummate wrecker and creator," the first developer-hero. Faust was a visionary, determined to deliver his society, through forced economic development on an epic scale, from what Marx called "the idiocy of rural life." That life had deep roots, and many ordinary lives were ruined as well as enriched by Faust's schemes. But unlike other modern developer-heroes—Peter the Great, Baron Haussman, Robert Moses—Faust agonized over the costs of modernization to those who get in the way.

Like all other forms of coercion, forced modernization generates defenses, most notably the ironies and ambivalences of Baudelaire, Dostoyevsky, and other literary modernists. Berman finds in Baudelaire a new aesthetic of upheaval, anonymity, and spectatorship. In Pushkin, Gogol, Dostoyevsky, and Mandelstam he traces a "modernism of underdevelopment," a whimsical or self-lacerating response to the grotesque unevenness of half-modern (e.g., 19th-century Russian, 20th-century Latin American) societies. And to bring it all back home (at least to those of us for whom the modern city is home), Berman discusses some varieties of modernism in the 20th century, especially in New York: the techno-pastoral fantasies of the Futurists and LeCorbusier, the "expressway world" envisioned by Robert Moses, and the urban-neighborhood-as-democratic-microcosm of Jane Jacobs.

Berman's primary metaphor for the whole vast modern experience is "the tragedy of development." This seems right. A tragedy is not an ordinary misfortune; it is a catastrophe that no one, not even its protagonist, could will to turn out differently, because its causation is ultimately bound up with those qualities or values that make the hero what he or she most deeply is. The dreadful dislocations of modernity, our confusion, insecurity, and homelessness, the forgetting or destruction of so many cherished pasts—these are the price we have paid for aspirations that most of us nevertheless will not give up: mobility, abundance, novelty, and above all, freedom from traditional pieties and superstitions. Modernity simultaneously evokes and frustrates our yearnings for more plentiful life. The capitalist market conjures up prodigies, harbingers of infinite delight, but in the form of commodities, which soon blight and decay. Yet to return to the pre-capitalist past would be, as Marx wrote, "to decree everlasting mediocrity."

Marx's solution to the dilemmas of modernity is more and deeper modernity—that is, socialism. "We know that to work well . . . these new forces of society want only to be mastered by new people—and such are the workers, as much the invention of modern times as machinery itself." Or as Berman puts it, wistfully: "The way beyond the contradictions will have to lead through modernity, not out of it. . . . We must start where we are: psychically naked, stripped of all religious, aesthetic, moral haloes and sentimental veils, thrown back on our individual will and energy, forced to exploit each other and ourselves in order to survive; and yet, in spite of all, thrown together by the same forces that pull us apart, dimly aware of all we might be together, ready to stretch ourselves to grasp new human possibilities, to develop identities and mutual bonds that can help us hold together as the fierce modern air blows hot and cold through us all."

The style of that passage is engaging, but the vision behind it has met with resistance from the anti-modernist left. To Berman's radical critics, like Jackson Lears, talk of capitalism as "tragedy" is so much feckless sentimentality. Modernization, they retort, is not an impersonal, world-historical progress but a novel form of class domination. The antagonists in the drama of modernity are not simply "the new" and "the old," but modernizing elites and subject populations. Modern culture is called forth and limited by the requirements of these modernizing elites. The ideal of personal "growth" is an ideological reflex, a rationalization of capitalism's need for unrestrained economic growth. The continual transformation of work and family life wrought by the expansion of markets and the pressures of competition appears to Berman as a "dialectic" of "innovative self-destruction." It appears to Lears as "the destructive power of capitalist 'progress,' which uproots people from kin and communal ties, transforming them into mobile, interchangeable units of 'human capital.'" What Berman celebrates as "our" quest for "more abundant life" Lears describes very differently: "Professional and managerial elites have sanitized and popularized the ideal of self-development" into "an anxious, calculating hedonism, well suited to the daily rhythms of routine and release under corporate capitalism." The result, according to Lears and Lasch, is not high tragedy and dialectical progress but a culture of narcissism.

The anti-modernists' solution is not, of course, a still deeper modernity. That way, they warn, lie collective amnesia, one-dimensionality, endless accommodation to centralized authority and the vicissitudes of capital accumulation. The illusions of individualism—unlimited "fulfillment" and untrammeled "liberation"—must be renounced. Only loyalty to something larger than the self—to family, community, religion, or craft—will make possible the limited but genuine autonomy of which humans are capable, will enable us to call on the past to judge the present. Tradition and transcendence are a mighty fortress, our bulwark against the encroachments of modern nihilism.

The utility of tradition is an old theme, though it's rarely expounded with the sophistication of Lears or Lasch. The burden of their argument is not nostalgia for a pre-modern past, but a useful reminder that the modern "adventure" is not predestined to a happy ending. Nihilism—whether as total collapse or total control—is a real possibility, something the greatest modern minds have always acknowledged: Marx, for example, soberly acknowledging that barbarism was a not implausible alternative to socialism, or D. H. Lawrence predicting "a wave of generosity or a wave of death."

Still, a warning is not a program. The anti-modernists are right to dispute the facile notion that traditional forms and values are merely instrumental, merely ways of keeping people in their place. But it is equally facile to suppose that the destruction of traditions is merely instrumental, merely a way of establishing new and more efficient forms of domination. Religious, kin, and communal loyalties do embody ineradicable human longings; but so, too, do modern impulses toward criticism, rebellion, autonomy, and pleasure, however grievously these impulses have been exploited or perverted. And as for transcendence—where to find it? Modernity may be no place of grace, but what if there *is* no such place? It's all very well for Lears to invoke Nietzsche's contempt for the "evasive banality" and "weightlessness" of modern culture, or William James's scorn for "the complacent bourgeois cult of material progress." But in the history of thought there are not two more wholly secular thinkers, more uncompromising and disenchanted refusers of the supernatural, than James and Nietzsche. Modernity may be a misfortune: who would not prefer enchantment to disenchantment? We would all, as Camus wrote in *The Myth of Sisyphus*, much prefer having something worth obeying to the prospect of sinning with impunity. But though our society and culture may crumble for lack of them, belief and loyalty cannot be willed.

Berman, for his part, never fully faces up to the possibility of nihilism. This failing may explain the relative absence of Nietzsche from *All That Is Solid Melts Into Air*. In *Beyond Good and Evil* everything solid really does melt into air: politics, morality, common sense, all evaporate before our bewildered gaze, in an atmosphere so rarefied that most of us can hardly breathe. And that, according to Nietzsche, is the key to the modern predicament: only the few, aristocrats by nature, can live without illusion, can endure the depths of modern irony. That irony exposes even scientific rationalism as a metaphysical prejudice, and secular humanism as an ethical prejudice. Finally, if one looks long enough into the abyss, Nietzsche writes, the abyss looks back. It sounds like an unnerving experience.

Berman is not unnerved. He is earnest, and a democrat. He writes: "To unmask phony claims of transcendence is to demand and fight for real transcendence. . . . We need to strive for that precarious, dynamic balance." This statement contains two generous assumptions: that there is a "real transcendence," and that it is available to all of "us." Nietzsche puts both these assumptions in question. Those of us who are not heroes or *Übermenschen* can only hope that Berman's assumptions are true. Still, it is an uncomfortable thought that the person who saw most deeply into the meaning of modernity was neither an optimist nor a democrat. Berman means to bring us comfort, and he does. But it, too, soon melts into air.

Tragedy and Utopia

Can the welfare state become a moral community? Unpacking this question requires asking several others. Are there needs—say for love, dignity, or achievement—for which no collective provision can be made? Can social policy treat people impersonally, as equals, and at the same time as individuals? Can any social bonds finally withstand the mobility and self-assertiveness fostered by a competitive market economy? Can our capacity for sympathy be enlarged without being diluted—can we really care about the needs of strangers?

Michael Ignatieff, a young Canadian economist and historian currently at King's College, Cambridge, has approached these questions by reflecting on some of the seminal texts of our culture: St Augustine's *Confessions*, Shakespeare's *King Lear*, Hume's *Enquiries*, Rousseau's *Discourse on Inequality*, Adam Smith's *The Wealth of Nations*, and others. This may sound like a surprisingly leisurely style of political argument at a moment when the welfare state is under attack in much of the English-speaking world; but in its way, Ignatieff's literate, engaging, unsystematic mediation* is very much to the point.

"The test of responsible political argument," Ignatieff writes, "is to know which needs can be satisfied through politics and which cannot." To help articulate this distinction, he offers a long and ingenious reading of that apparently unpolitical tragedy, *King Lear*. Lear's gradual, appalling reduction to a "poor, bare forked animal," to "unaccommodated man," is a parable of the relationship between identity and entitlement. What Lear learns on the heath, according to Ignatieff, is the futility of asking strangers to "reason not the need," that is, to accord us the dignity of accepting our own estimate of our needs.

The Needs of Strangers, Viking, 1983.

Partly through his willfulness, Lear has estranged his daughters. When he demands a retinue, he is treated in turn like a stranger, a "basest beggar," admonished not to take his desires for needs and informed that others can better determine his needs than he can.

For a king, this indignity is tragic. For the dependents of the modern welfare state, it is routine. But there is logic in it: the acknowledgment of need creates a corresponding obligation, so allowing people to define their own needs is, to that extent, allowing them to define the obligations of others. That sort of trust can subsist within families; but outside them, on the vast bureaucratic heath of the welfare state, its survival is problematic. For administrative purposes, need must be distinguished from desire and trust replaced by policy.

In the history of thinking about need and desire, St. Augustine figures prominently. Augustine's early life was free of all deprivations except one: spiritual restlessness. This experience produced his famous conception of the City of God, where our freedom to choose, the negative freedom of the secular city, would be completed by Grace, the certainty that we have chosen our true good. Augustine anticipated and recoiled from what Ignatieff calls "the loneliness and anguish of modern secular freedom." At the center of his political psychology was our need for meaning and certainty—for what Nietzsche would later call "metaphysical comfort." But no secular political order, then or now, could provide for this fundamental need, whence Augustine's haunting pronouncement: *non habemus hic manentem civitatem*; here below is no lasting community.

Shakespeare and Augustine created memorable images of anomie: the heath and the City of Man. In these they expressed their own and their culture's conviction that for unaffiliated men and women, not guarded by familial love or guided by traditional wisdom, life would be unbearable and community impossible. This immemorial pessimism was challenged during the Enlightenment, most persuasively by David Hume and Adam Smith. Hume's exemplary life and legendary death, as well as his writings, were an argument for the sufficiency of the secular. Having doubted every metaphysical certainty and demonstrated that reason itself was necessarily "the slave of the passions," Hume affirmed that social solidarity was nevertheless possible, through the cultivation of "benevolence"—for Hume, one of the most important of "the passions." This affirmation, Hume's celebrated skepticism notwithstanding, presupposed a fundamental faith: that the energies released by the demise of traditional superstitions would enable ordinary men and women to attain self-confidence and self-control. If allowed, as never before in history, to define their own needs, they would find that one of those needs was for the sympathy and affection of others—even strangers.

They would also find, as they entered the newly-forming market economy, that their own needs and the needs of strangers formed a kind of system—Hume actually dubbed the capitalist economy a "system of needs." The great philosopher of this new system, Adam Smith, argued that strangers could best satisfy one another's needs not by direct public action but by engaging in a global division of labor based on competitive advantage. For Smith, progress toward prosperity, even for the poorest, depended crucially on inequality and on what Ignatieff calls "the blind upward spiral of need." Only a society in which need is defined as whatever people want rather than what the community decrees is good or sufficient for them will release their full powers of ingenuity and industry. Admittedly, what people want—especially well-off people—may prove vulgar and frivolous, considering the urgent needs of desperate strangers. But the worldly and practical Smith had his own robust faith: in the competitive abilities of ordinary men and women as well as (perhaps naively) in the generosity and civic-mindedness of the successful.

Rousseau's rejection of these individualist assumptions was, according to Ignatieff, a momentous event in Western intellectual history. While Rousseau's description of market society—emphasizing the division of labor, geographical mobility, technical innovation, the profusion of commodities, the dissolution and recreation of status hierarchies—largely corresponded to Smith's, his moral evaluation was profoundly different. Smith believed that market relations would to some extent evoke, and to an even greater extent reduce the need for, social solidarity. Rousseau feared that a world of strangers would be a world not of self-regulating harmony but of envy, insecurity, insincerity, and alienation. In place of what Hume called the "great scramble" of commercial society, Rousseau proposed a republic of virtue, in which, as Ignatieff puts it, citizens would "democratically decide upon some form of collective constraint on the inequalities of fortune."

Rousseau's originality lay in his insight into the psychology of possessive individualism and in his application of classical political morality to the construction of an ideal modern republic. He was the first anti-capitalist utopian. But his theory failed, Ignatieff claims, because "societies that constrain the economic desires of their citizens . . . and that try to make the distribution of wealth and income a matter of collective choice, risk economic stagnation" and jeopardize political liberty. More generally, utopians deny the intractable conflict of need with need; they suppose, says Ignatieff, that "the human good is without internal contradiction." They try to eliminate tragedy from history.

Tragedy, Ignatieff replies, cannot be eliminated from history. He is surely right. But is he right that this is what utopians invariably seek, and that the modern welfare state is about the best we can hope for? In arriving at this conclusion, Ignatieff is particularly hard on, and uncharacteristically imperceptive about, Marx. While granting Marx's fundamental criticism—that the 18th-century ideal of capitalist prosperity "has required all the violence and domination of imperial power in order to come true"—he charges that Marx went on to prescribe a final "destination for the tragic spiral of human need" and thus succumbed to "a fantasy of deliverance from history." "Marx," he writes, "is largely silent about the natural and unalterable elements of our destiny, and it was upon this silence that his utopia was built."

This is a misunderstanding. Like Freud, Marx sought only to deliver humankind from needless misery to inevitable unhappiness. In the *Economic and Philosophical Manuscripts*, commonly considered his most naively utopian work, he envisioned this alternative to the tyranny of money:

> Assume man to be man [ie, not *homo economicus*] and his relationship to the world to be a human one: then you can exchange love only for love, trust for trust, etc. If you want to enjoy art, you must be an artistically cultivated person; if you want to influence others, then you must be a person with a stimulating and encouraging effect on them. Every one of your relations to man and nature must be a specific expression . . . of your real, individual life. If you love without evoking love in return—that is, if your loving does not produce reciprocal love; if through a living expression of yourself as a loving person you do not make yourself a loved person—then your love is impotent and a misfortune.

Implicit in this passage is a definition of utopia: not the elimination of tragedy, but its universalization. When each person's sufferings and failures—her fate—are individual, rather than circumstantial and accidental, as is so often the case in the "great scramble," then no more can be required of politics. The democratization of tragedy is surely a modest enough conception of utopia. But it is a long way from the contemporary welfare state.

Consuming Passions

In his lovely idyll *The Soul of Man Under Socialism*, Oscar Wilde dreamed a happy ending to the travails of modernity:

> At present machinery competes against man. Under proper conditions machinery will serve man. There is no doubt at all that this is the future of machinery; and just as trees grow while the country gentleman sleeps, so while humanity will be amusing itself, or enjoying cultivated leisure—which, and not labour, is the end of man—or making beautiful things, or simply contemplating the world with admiration and delight, machinery will be doing all the necessary and unpleasant work. . . . On mechanical slavery, on the slavery of the machine, the future of the world depends.

It has not turned out that way, of course; at least not yet. Things are still in the saddle, riding humankind. But though the grinding Victorian poverty that appalled Wilde has not entirely disappeared, it has by and large evolved, in the developed capitalist world, into something less stark, though perhaps no less invidious: consumer society. The "realm of necessity," of want, that Marx deplored has been succeeded not by a "realm of freedom" but by something intermediate: a realm of commodities. Life is less brutish and short, but the grandest promises of technological modernity—individual autonomy, creative work, "cultivated leisure"—have not been fulfilled for most people. "Progress," the common expectation of 19th century liberals and socialists, has taken a queer turn. Consumer society is not exactly what anyone expected or hoped for. It is by no means the antithesis of the good society; rather, it's a more or less plausible counterfeit.

A great deal of American social criticism in this century has been a response to the advent of consumerism. Some of this criticism has taken the form of sentimental moralizing:

lamentations over the emptiness of affluence, the perils of prosperity, the failure of "success." Some of it has been more serious: academic (Erving Goffman) or popular (Vance Packard) or
conservative (Daniel Bell) or utopian (Paul Goodman) critiques
of mass society. More recently, taking a clue from the Frank-
furt School of social theorists (including Herbert Marcuse) and
from British cultural historians Raymond Williams and E. P.
Thompson, American radicals have tried to understand consumer society in all its complexity. Which is to say, not as a fall
from grace or a capitalist conspiracy or the inevitable unfolding of the dialectic of modernity but as a tense compromise
between the requirements of the powerful and the aspirations
of the ruled.

Christopher Lasch has pioneered this approach. Although
often mistaken for conservative nostalgia, Lasch's work is an
acute and potentially subversive analysis of the deep structure
of social control in developed capitalist societies. A younger
historian, Jackson Lears, took up a similar problem in *No Place
of Grace: Antimodernism and the Transformation of American
Culture, 1880–1929*, published in 1981. Lears's widely praised
study argued that American culture underwent a crisis at the
end of the 19th century in response to increasing secularization, technological and demographic changes, and the rise of
a national market economy. The result of this crisis was a nor-
mative shift from the "bourgeois ethos," enjoining "perpetual
work, compulsive saving, civic responsibility, and a rigid morality of self-denial" to a "therapeutic ethos," which sanctioned
"periodic leisure, compulsive spending, apolitical passivity,
and an apparently permissive (but subtly coercive) morality
of individual fulfillment." What made *No Place of Grace* original was Lears's further contention that "the older culture was
suited to a production-oriented society of small entrepreneurs;
the newer culture epitomized a consumption-oriented society
dominated by bureaucratic corporations."

Lears has returned to the subject, this time in the company
of five other radical historians. *The Culture of Consumption:*

Critical Essays in American History, 1880–1890,* edited by Lears and Richard Wightman Fox, tries to document the shift from a "producer ethic" to a "consumer ethic" through six studies of individuals and institutions within the American cultural elite. It is a superb collection: wide-ranging, detailed, and suggestive. Lears leads off with a study of the early history of advertising, ca. 1880–1930. He claims that the spread and refinement of advertising strategies did not merely follow from changes in popular values; on the other hand, neither did it create or effortlessly manipulate them. Secularization, urbanization, and the shift from entrepreneurial to corporate capitalism had left many people with a diminished or fragmented sense of self and a longing for more "real" or intense experience. Advertisers rushed to satisfy (i.e., exploit) these needs, but often out of a sense of public service, or at least with a sincere belief in their own prophecies of abundance and promises of self-realization. Very revealing on this score is Lears's portrait of Bruce Barton, a leading advertiser and whose career embodied many of the confusions that gave rise to the therapeutic ethos.

The growth of advertising influenced another key institution of consumer culture: mass-circulation magazines. However genteel or elitist they may have been, Victorian literary magazines generally treated their readers as peers, without condescension, and they reflected a traditional notion of reading as a contemplative activity. Christopher Wilson's essay traces the development of a new editorial "voice" and rhetoric imported from the sphere of advertising and marketing by a new type of editor-manager. Pre-tested and pre-promoted, these magazines—*McClure's, Saturday Evening Post, Ladies' Home Journal*, and others—combined ersatz realism, pseudo-intimacy, and predictability to create a streamlined, "managed" reading experience. They became ideal marketing vehicles, not merely for individual products but for consumerist values and self-images.

Two essays in *The Culture of Consumption* are biographical.

*Pantheon, 1983.

Richard Fox recounts the frustrated, poignant career of Robert Lynd, sociologist, reformer, and author of *Middletown*, a classic portrait of small-town America in the mid-1920s. Lynd began as a religious radical and a harsh critic of corporate power. But as he elaborated his critique of consumer culture, he was captured by one of its central assumptions: that ordinary men and women are largely passive, impulsive, and manipulable and therefore need the guiding expertise of trained, caring social scientists and professional planners. For all his idealism, Lynd ended by helping to foster among American intellectuals an undemocratic and self-serving conception: the "rational," scientifically ordered, bureaucratically managed society.

Jean-Christophe Agnew's essay on Henry James is the best in the collection. Agnew's perceptive review of commercial metaphors in James's fiction, and of ambivalence about American business civilization in James's memoirs, is prefaced by a dazzling methodological essay. According to Agnew, commodities have always carried social meanings, but when they rapidly and incessantly "improve" or obsolesce, social meanings become unstable. Contemporary advertising "defamiliarizes" once-familiar objects and their customary attributes, and the result is a "fragmentation of needs," entailing a subtle but widespread social disorientation. Consumers try to cope with this confusion by constructing a symbolic "code" made up of commodities, the way primitive peoples orient themselves in an incomprehensible and threatening environment by constructing myths and rituals. Agnew's brief sketch hints at how an anthropology of consumer culture might be constructed—a keenly interesting question for all of us who live in one.

The last two essays in the book have contemporary subjects. Robert Westbrook examines the commodification of American politics, arguing that the electoral relationship "has become of packages to packages, a relationship shaped by managers who are themselves for sale." He outlines the history of professional campaign management, which by now consists of identifying and canvassing an "audience package" and then assembling and promoting a "candidate package" for that audience's (i.e., electorate's) consumption. As a result, electoral politics, like other forms of mass marketing, reinforces the apathy, atomization, and spectatorship that are endemic in consumer societies.

Finally, Michael Smith depicts the United States as a "triumph of commodity scientism." In daily life in the 20th century, large-scale technology has become, for most people, indispensable but incomprehensible. Public attitudes toward new technological ventures like the arms race and the space race have been engineered by "presentation strategies" that play on anxieties (especially among males) about powerlessness—loss of technical competence, of control over one's personal environment, even of sexual prowess. Automobile advertising early on perfected the simple trick of transferring or projecting attributes from product to consumer—for example, the car's power implies the driver's virility, its efficiency his purposefulness, its technical complexity his technical literacy, and so on. Government public-relations experts took over this approach to sell the Apollo moon flight, an expensive, wasteful project useful mainly as Cold War propaganda. The success of the moon shot generated national feelings of prowess and mastery, which masked the actual lack of public debate and control over the whole venture and over technological development generally.

The Culture of Consumption documents the invasion of nearly every spere of modern American culture—journalism, literature, social science, politics, technology—by therapeutic attitudes, consumerist values, and advertising and mass-market techniques. But if this is an invasion, who is the aggressor? To their credit the authors recognize that that's not a simple question. They have avoided the temptation to explain consumerism as a gigantic fraud, a capitalist plot to mystify and pacify the populace. The populace has often enough pursued commodities actively, and elites have often believed in (and sometimes even been victimized by) the ideologies they purvey.

Still, consumerism has undeniably had political consequences: it has promoted popular passivity and the centralization of decision-making power in the state executive and in large bureaucratic corporations. If this process is not a result of deliberate ruling-class manipulation, then how to account for it? *The Culture of Consumption* does not answer that question, but it does contain a useful hint. Several contributors cite Raymond Williams's fine essay "Advertising: The Magic System" (from *Problems in Materialism and Culture*), which defines consumer society as "a cultural pattern in which objects must be validated, if only in fantasy, by association with social and personal meanings which in a different [e.g., socialist] cultural pattern might be more directly available." This "validation" is accomplished by a sort of magic: since individual consumption "leaves whole areas of human need unsatisfied, the attempt is made, by magic, to associate this consumption with human desires to which it has no real reference . . . [desires for] social respect, good taste, health, beauty, success, power to control your environment. The magic obscures the real sources of general satisfaction because their discovery would involve a radical change in the whole common way of life." Need is subversive; it must be bewitched.

Like all successful sorcerers, the ideologists of consumer culture believe in their own magic. "Fundamentally," writes Williams, "they are involved with the rest of the society in the magical confusion to which the magical gestures are a response." Sincerity is, after all, a requisite of effective propaganda. And besides, the ideology of consumption, of fulfillment through individual marketplace transactions, is plausible. How many other sources of fulfillment are there, for most of us?

Altered slightly—say, to "what other sources of fulfillment *could* there be?"—that question is a radical one and invites utopian answers, like Wilde's. The contributors to *The Culture of Consumption* decline this invitation; their book is diagnostic, not programmatic. In particular, they resist any suggestions that the dilemmas created by economic and technological "progress" will be resolved through more of the same, or that "genuine" progress lies just beyond the next turn of the modernist dialectic. They are anti-modernists, convinced that modernization erodes vital (though flawed) traditions of socialism, self-help, and mutual aid; of family, neighborhood, religion, and craft.

It is tempting to equate anti-modernism with nostalgia, though the authors would reject that suggestion too. Still, some of them do occasionally slip into ambiguous usages. Lears and Fox write that in a corporate economy, most workers can "no longer" aspire to become their own bosses—but could they ever, in any important sense, considering the harsh constraints imposed by pre-modern technology? Westbrook hopes for a "revival" of republican democracy. Smith regrets that contemporary Americans have become "more" removed from decisions about technology's social uses. The authors admit that mass consumption has lightened old burdens and furnished new pleasures. But they hint that the price has been too high: that pre-modern society was fundamentally more democratic and allowed more of the reality (though less of the rhetoric) of individual autonomy.

If that large historical claim is true (and I'm not persuaded of it), then what is to be done? Few people seriously propose a return to the "producer ethic," even if the conditions in which that ethic flourished (an accumulating, entrepreneurial capitalism) could somehow be recreated. And surely no one (well, perhaps William F. Buckley) wants the feudal ethic back. Whatever wisdom those cultures embodied will have to find a new form.

In their introduction to *The Culture of Consumption* Lears and Fox write: "People deserve a more democratic as well as a more affluent way of life. That belief unites the authors of these six essays." Democracy plus affluence does indeed seem utopia enough for now. But though our six authors are emphatic about how not to get there, they are enigmatic about how we can. We will apparently have to wait for Lasch, Lears, and others on the anti-modernist left to work out a program as compelling as their critique. Perhaps they'll succeed in summoning ancient wisdom to rescue us beleaguered, bewitched moderns.

A Prophet, Honored

Christopher Lasch, who died recently, was arguably the most important American social critic in recent decades, and perhaps also the most unpalatable. In a series of important books, Lasch conducted an idiosyncratic, multidisciplinary, and disturbingly plausible polemic against the Enlightenment image of human development. The essence of enlightened moral psychology is universalism—the progressive, potentially unlimited extension of sympathy or imaginative identification beyond the local and traditional—as well as disinterestedness—the ability to weigh the happiness of distant others equally with one's own and that of one's familiars. Lasch demurred. For him, the limits imposed by infantile dependence, territoriality, scarcity, and mortality define human nature. To accept these intractable, immemorial limits and resolve to live a life of virtue and self-control within them is true wisdom and such happiness as we are capable of. Only an "arduous, even a tragic, understanding of life" makes maturity, efficacy, and heroism possible. An understanding, that is, of "the inescapability of evil in the form of natural limits on human freedom; the sinfulness of man's rebellion against those limits; and the moral value of work, which at once signifies man's submission to necessity and enables him to transcend it."

Genuine rootedness, Lasch argued, entails particular, parochial loyalties, and as a result, frequent conflict among members of a large society rather than rational allegiance to the social whole and disinterested universal cooperation. What makes for psychic health and strength is local identification and primal memory, an orientation to the past rather than to the future. In *The Culture of Narcissism* (1978) and *The Minimal Self* (1984), Lasch showed that the growing child urgently needs to experience both love and discipline from the same source, and that wage labor and mass production, which made this impossible by removing the father from the home, gave rise to a culture of narcissism. In *The True and Only Heaven* (1991), he broadened the diagnosis, identifying capitalism with modernity, which he describes as an all-out war on the past, individual and collective.

Unlike theological and metaphysical critiques of modernity, this secular psychoanalytic one undeniably has something in it. The infant's and child's outsized fantasies—of omnipotence and terrified helplessness, of rage and undifferentiated union, and so on—must gradually be worn down, reduced to human scale. And this inward, intensive identification—different from the outward-turning, assimilative identification that enlarges our sympathies—is what gives us human shape, psychically speaking, along with other, secondary identifications of the same sort: with church, neighborhood, and ethnic group. The memories of which these local identifications consist constitute us. We are our histories, in a way even more precise and intimate than previously appreciated.

On this understanding of psychoanalytic theory, late and distant attachments of the kind produced by sympathy can rarely equal, much less replace, earlier ones. And "a ruthless criticism of all things existing" (Marx's *echt*-modernist motto) will almost invariably encounter resistance even more tenacious than any based on economic self-interest. The theological, philosophical, and commonsense justifications of traditional prejudice and superstition have been largely swept away. But there seems to be another, evolutionary justification. For evolution apparently dictates that in order to mature, we have to master our imagination when young by binding or investing fantasy within nearby, particular entities. And many of us will not have much imaginative capacity left over later in life for modernist purposes.

This is discouraging. But perhaps not conclusively so, in a longer view. For what does "mature" mean? It means a personality strong enough to endure the stresses that begin when the developmental period ends and adulthood begins. In theory, extending the developmental period would allow the loosening of primary attachments and the incorporation of remoter, more general ones. And this is just what mass higher education in modern societies seems to have accomplished. Intellectual emancipation and political idealism may result as much from simply postponing adulthood as from enlightened or "subversive" pedagogy.

But while the gradual loosening of primary attachments is one thing, their rapid, wholesale destruction is another. All too often "modernity" has meant nothing more than the assault of capitalism on tradition, with enlightenment nowhere in view. Commodification, wage labor, and mass production have drastically undermined craft, regional, ethnic, religious, and even familial loyalties and virtues, substituting only the abstract disciplines of the market. Industrial capitalism may be readier than traditional societies to reward the distinctive virtues of modernity—intellectual curiosity, originality, tolerance, social solidarity—but it does little to foster them. The result is an unanchored moral culture: shallow, fragile, manipulative, in a word, narcissistic.

Modernity without enlightenment is a prescription for nihilism. Pre-modernity, both psychic and political, must be outgrown rather than merely suppressed, as industrial capitalism tends to do. On the other hand, it is arguably only developed industrial capitalism that allows a society the economic luxury of postponing adulthood, whether through higher education, travel, or some other vocational moratorium. Between these constraints, it is difficult to see any clear path to a secular, democratic-socialist utopia. Lasch's uniquely broad and deep critique of modernity has not convinced most of his readers. But it seems to lie squarely in the path of those who take the desirability of large-scale production, political cosmopolitanism, and religious and moral skepticism for granted. That is, nearly all of us.

A Farewell to Virtue

As one eases, or oozes, into middle age, one finds oneself reflecting rather more often than formerly that the world is going to hell in a handbasket. At any rate, one inclines a more sympathetic ear to the literature of cultural complaint. Those of us currently approaching cultural curmudgeonhood are fortunate: two splendid specimens have arrived this publishing season to confirm our suspicions, articulate our fears, fortify our dislikes, and generally provide a grim good time.

Gertrude Himmelfarb is the grande dame of American neoconservatism. An eminent historian, she is also the wife of neoconservative pope Irving Kristol and the mother of high-level Republican strategist William Kristol. Having produced several distinguished books on 19th-century English intellectual history, she has in recent years devoted herself to learnedly scolding late-20th-century Americans. *On Looking Into the Abyss: Untimely Thoughts on Culture and Society* (1993) warned that we are sliding toward moral and intellectual perdition. Since Nietzsche revealed its existence a century ago, "the abyss has grown deeper and more perilous, with new and more dreadful terrors lurking at the bottom. The beasts of modernism have mutated into the beasts of postmodernism—relativism into nihilism, amorality into immorality, irrationality into insanity, sexual deviancy into polymorphous perversity." Heidegger, Derrida, De Man, Rorty, and their deconstructionist epigones "may ultimately subvert liberal democracy together with all the other priggish metaphysical notions about truth, morality, and reality."

The title essay of Himmelfarb's new volume, *The De-Moralization of Society: From Victorian Virtues to Modern Values**,

*Knopf, 1994.

describes in sour detail what those "beasts of postmodernism" have wrought. Illegitimacy, divorce, crime, drug use, functional illiteracy, welfare dependency, and other negative social indicators have all increased in the last few decades, most of them dramatically. Just as dramatically, these indicators declined from the early to the late Victorian period. The social sinew and moral tone of the Victorian era were more robust than ours, Himmelfarb claims.

The reason for this demoralization, she argues, is our "demoralization": the erosion of the rigorous and unquestioned code of conduct that our forebears lived by. The much-derided "bourgeois virtues"—responsibility, respectability, sobriety, self-discipline, etc.—were indispensable to civic health. They still are, she claims, but our misguided present-day insistence on "value-free" administrative language and procedures, our reluctance to "impose" our morality through law and education, our overemphasis on rights and underemphasis on duties, our indifference (especially among cultural elites) to religious and other traditions, have left us without moral antibodies. The result is rampant social pathology.

All this sounds a good deal like Allan Bloom and William Bennett (though Himmelfarb is a better writer than either). And like Bloom and Bennett, it sends many liberals and leftists into paroxysms of irritation. Nevertheless, she is on to something. Our social fabric is indeed fraying. Most of Himmelfarb's book is given over not to denouncing the present age but to illustrating the practice of virtue among the Victorians. The contrast is poignant and persuasive. For all their intolerance, hypocrisy, and rigidity, the Victorian middle classes were, compared with us, more earnest, conscientious, self-confident, and self-sacrificing. They were better stewards of their world.

So what happened? How have we been "de-moralized"? Here is where I, at least, part company with the neoconservatives. Fundamentally, they have no other explanation for our malaise than a vast loss of moral nerve, a global change of intellectual climate. We must, they exhort us, come to our senses, pull up our socks, have faith, and ignore those irresponsible chattering skeptics. But that is no explanation and no solution.

I don't know of anyone who has a plausible explanation, except Christopher Lasch. Lasch, who died last year, authored two classic jeremiads, *The Culture of Narcissism: American Life in an Age of Diminishing Expectations* (1979) and *The True and Only Heaven: Progress and Its Critics* (1991) His posthumous essay collection, *The Revolt of the Elites and the Betrayal of Democracy* (1995) while not a landmark work, contains plenty of vintage Lasch.

Lasch's description of our plight resembles the neoconservatives' in many respects, notably in his emphasis on the decay of civic virtue. But his diagnosis goes far deeper than theirs. American democracy, he points out, flourished in the 18th- and 19th-century environment of proprietorship, small-scale production, and the broad diffusion of wealth. It was these conditions that called forth the "democratic habits" of self-reliance, responsibility, and initiative; it was they, more than any religious or moral doctrine, that produced "character" and "virtue." And it was not primarily religious or moral skepticism but mass production and political centralization which undermined that character and made those habits superfluous.

It was, in a word, capitalism. The independent farmer, artisan, or shopkeeper required one kind of character and psychology; the wage laborer another. The 19th-century Populist revolt against capitalism was far more widespread and more radical than any opposition mounted by the industrial working class, precisely because it aimed at defending a way of life and a psychic ecology rather than merely improving wages and working conditions. The Populists were defeated, and the ensuing integration of the national economy and centralization of state power are largely responsible for—to use a phrase Lasch made famous two decades ago—"the narcissistic personality of our time": shallow, fragile, manipulative, dependent, conformist, and helpless to resist the blandishments of consumer culture.

This is Lasch's great achievement: to have shown that the moral psychology of capitalism is profoundly different from what is claimed by either its apologists or its detractors. Unsurprisingly, this achievement is not much appreciated by his fellow cultural complainers, most of whom are political conservatives with no stomach for railing against godless capitalism. Contemporary conservatives, as Russell Jacoby (author of *Dogmatic Wisdom*, another splendid contribution to the literature of cultural complaint) observes, "worship the market and bemoan the [culture] it engenders."

Lasch, it must be admitted, has no solution to the dilemma he so brilliantly elucidates. In *The Revolt of the Elites* he alludes to "the probing social commentary that took shape in the latter half of the nineteenth century, when it became evident that small property was disappearing and people began to ask themselves whether the virtues associated with proprietorship could be preserved, in some other form, under economic conditions that seemed to make proprietorship untenable." In *The True and Only Heaven* he expounds those writings at length but finally acknowledges that while contemporary populists "call for small-scale production and political decentralization . . . they do not explain how these objectives can be achieved in a modern economy."

Perhaps they can't be achieved. In that case, it's farewell to virtue, however eloquently anyone complains.

Can We Be Good Without God?

There seems to be a connection, historical and perhaps even logical, between metaphysics and morality; that is, between views about the nature of being or knowledge and views about justice and the good. A vague sense (which is surely all that most of us have) of this connection is one thing, however; an original, rigorous, and comprehensive historical account is something else again—an immense achievement. Yet this is only one feature of Charles Taylor's monumental book. *Sources of the Self** bears out, to some extent at least, a seemingly extravagant compliment proffered by Richard Rorty in reviewing Taylor's *Collected Papers*: "He is attempting nothing less than a synthesis of moral reflection with intellectual history, one which will do for our time what Hegel did for his." Here is Taylor's own statement of his aims:

> "[T]o write and articulate a history of the modern identity . . . to designate the ensemble of (largely unarticulated) understandings of what it is to be a human agent: the senses of inwardness, freedom, individuality, and being embedded in nature which are at home in the modern West . . . to show how the ideals and interdicts of this identity—what it casts in relief and what it casts in shadow—shape our philosophical thought, our epistemology and our philosophy of language, largely without our awareness."

Not quite so grand as Hegel's, perhaps, but ambitious enough.

What is the "modern identity"? Whatever else may characterize it, at least three elements do. First, inwardness, or the understanding of our selfhood not as externally defined by the privileges and duties of our station or our relation to

Sources of the Self: The Making of the Modern Identity by Charles Taylor. Harvard University Press, 1989.

the overall order of being, but as something attained through turning inward, taking a reflexive stance, exploring our inner structures, resources, or depths. Second, the belief that ordinary life—work, friendship, marriage and the family—is our proper sphere and an adequate source of meaning and fulfillment rather than the ignoble lot of those not up to the ascetic, contemplative, or military virtues of saint, sage, and warrior-aristocrat. Third, expressivism, or recourse to nature and the feelings it evokes in us as a spiritual and moral counterweight to analytic, instrumental reason.

Taylor narrates the history of philosophy (in some cases also of theology, literary theory, and modern literature) in relation to the gradual emergence of each of these elements. For example: according to Plato, correct perception of the cosmic order makes possible self-knowledge and control of the passions; reason is the source of morality and happiness. Augustine modifies Plato's conception: rather than employing dialectic to arrive at the Idea of the Good, the soul reflects on its activities and powers and recognizes God as their source. Descartes turns inward, looking not for God but for intellectual certainty and moral dignity. In Descartes' successors, especially Locke and Kant, this reflexivity or inward turn is further radicalized and secularized. By the end of Taylor's account, what had seemed merely a sequence of philosophical positions now appears as a vast drama whose upshot is us.

Here's another narrative. The triumph of Enlightenment rationalism meant an increased sense of individual autonomy and dignity, of what Taylor calls "self-responsible freedom." But at the same time, the decline of belief in Divine Providence and the new scientific view of nature as inert matter, a mechanism subject to rigid laws, threatened the loss of perennial spiritual and moral resources. According to Taylor, Kant's concept of morality as an aspect of human rational agency, a "secularized variant of *agape* implicit in reason itself," and the Romantic "notion of an inner voice or impulse, the idea that we find the truth within us, and in particular in our feelings," were both responses to this threatened loss, attempts to supply the defects of the culture's newly forming identity. In Taylor's tale of Western intellectual history as the evolution of an identity, in his ability to bring the most diverse cultural developments into his story line, there really is something reminiscent of Hegel. And fortunately, unlike Hegel, he writes lucid prose.

The scope, complexity, and ingenuity of Taylor's arguments make them difficult to summarize except in drastically compressed form (like my last two paragraphs). Detailed discussions of ancient and seventeenth-century philosophy, Renaissance Neo-Platonism, Reformation spirituality, Montaigne, Kant, Deism, the Enlightenment, the German Romantics, Schopenhauer, Baudelaire, Dostoevsky, Nietzsche, Rilke, and Pound, among other topics and writers, are carefully woven into the narrative tapestry. And Taylor fully acknowledges that the history of ideas cannot by itself explain the large shifts in outlook he is tracking; several brief but sensible observations about historical causation dispel any misgivings on this score.

More fruitful than further summary of Taylor's historical epic might be a look at some of his philosophical premises and moral judgments. *Sources of the Self* is a work of scrupulous but not at all detached scholarship; it is intensely purposeful. Like virtually everyone else nowadays, Taylor is worried about modernity. The core of the modern identity, the essence of modernity, is scientific rationality. The application (in Taylor's view, the misapplication) of the axioms and methods of the natural sciences to epistemology, ethics, psychology and the social sciences—a tendency he calls "naturalism" and plausibly claims is standard procedure in those fields—has, he believes, obstructed our access to our traditions and depleted our moral resources.

A common enough theme, to which Taylor brings uncommon philosophical skills. His earlier writings, particularly *Hegel,* showed him in command of both the Anglo-American and Continental traditions—among academic philosophers, Taylor is considered a "bridge" figure. In the two volumes of

Collected Papers and the first hundred pages of *Sources of the Self* he draws on the work of Merleau-Ponty, Heidegger, and Wittgenstein to construct a critique of, and alternative to, naturalism.

What is, or is supposed to be, the "scientific" attitude toward morality? Most fundamentally, perhaps, that values are not "real," that judgments about good and bad are not "objective"; they are preferences, which can be explained or interpreted, adjusted if one was mistaken about relevant facts or modified in response to new feelings and experiences, but not justified, not proved true or false. From this follows a conception of moral philosophy as neutral and procedural: its purpose is not to expound the nature of the Good or of virtue but to work out social and interpersonal rules, institutions, decision-procedures that will seem fair and just to most people, whatever their values or their vision of the good life. Both utilitarianism and rights-based liberalism, probably the most common varieties of political philosophy in the English-speaking world, presuppose this value neutrality.

In the social sciences, naturalism prescribes striving for intersubjective validity. Data that only the subject can testify to, that can't be recorded by and read off some instrument, and theories that require informal, unspecifiable qualities of imagination or judgment to apply—these don't count.

Taylor objects that naturalism's methodological restrictions have impoverished philosophy and social theory, and thereby public life. Neutralism about values inevitably slides over into subjectivism, the glib dismissal of all values as "fictitious," or relativism, the equally mindless acceptance of all values as equally valid and beyond rational adjudication. Individualism slides into atomism, the denial that some common good, over and above the goals of individuals or aggregates, may rightly command a person's loyalty, even obedience.

On the contrary, Taylor argues, moral theory can't be neutral, because a person's identity cannot be specified without reference to her or his commitments, stance, values. The proof of this gets a little technical but is, roughly: we are what we say about ourselves to our language community, what we answer to the question, "Who am I?" This always involves saying what we most deeply care about or aspire to. What matters most to us is what matters most about us.

Politically, too, the individual is constituted in and through a community. The rights and desires of liberal and utilitarian theory are only intelligible, can only be exercised, in communities of a certain sort. Since the survival and flourishing of such communities is a precondition of our fulfilling (or even having) those rights and desires, a commitment to the former takes precedence over asserting the latter.

Once again, I've offered a highly compressed rendering of an enormously complex argument. At this point, however, instead of adding qualifications, I'd like to simplify—to get down and dirty. Something about Taylor's tremendously impressive effort rubs me the wrong way. It's not Taylor himself; his is a dignified but friendly, on the whole quite likable, authorial voice. And while others may find fault with his treatment of Platonism, Puritanism, Romanticism, or modernism, I cannot. Perhaps it's just impossible not to resent a forceful challenge to some of one's most cherished beliefs. Taylor manages to shake my faith without quite converting me—yes, I admit it: I'm a naturalist.

Not, of course, a fundamentalist or even an orthodox one. I don't believe that science can, or ever will, explain all human behavior, or that all values are illusory. I'm comfortable with entities and explanations above the molecular level. I'm not, that is, a flaming positivist or a roaring reductionist. But I do think that where a naturalistic (neurochemical, sociobiological, psychoanalytic, economic) explanation for someone's belief or behavior seems adequate, it may well be adequate; and that while "community" is an indispensable political metaphor (and communitarianism has something going for it), it is, in the end, only a metaphor. I'm a pragmatic naturalist. Usually, in fact, I just say "pragmatist," but Taylor's harsh strictures elicited a stubborn residual allegiance to the old, outworn creed.

For one thing, there is his too-sweeping disparagement of naturalistic social science. Not that I have much use for present-day quantitative academic social science: on the contrary. Still, I feel Taylor ought, just by virtue of being so astute and influential a critic, to disavow the sentimental tosh frequently talked about the uniqueness and ineffability of human beings and the preposterousness, even perversity, of behaviorism. Behaviorism works, after all: in prisons, police states, marketing strategies, and electoral campaigns, just to name some of the main institutions and modes of social control in modern societies. True, it did not work in *Walden Two*, because there Skinner proposed a subtler, nobler goal than eliciting or suppressing discrete, overt behaviors over a limited span. But if the latter is all you want a "science of behavior" for, then a perfectly adequate one is available to you, notwithstanding the ineffable depth and complexity of human beings when they are treated like human beings. As always, what counts as truth depends on one's purpose.

This is a quibble, however, compared with the issues raised by Taylor's moral theory. One of Taylor's central claims in *Sources of the Self*—it is almost a leitmotif—is that a naturalistic ethic like utilitarianism or Marxism is "confused" and "deeply incoherent" (the deadliest of philosophical epithets) in one crucial respect: all such theories presuppose in practice some moral value or ideal, like universal and impartial benevolence in the case of the *philosophes* and Benthamites, social justice in the case of Marxists, or simply, in the most general case, to reduce suffering, while in principle denying that any such value is other than an arbitrary, subjective preference. Pressed repeatedly and persuasively, this claim made me first uncomfortable, then defiant. For suppose it is true? It may be that my moral heroes—Godwin and Bentham, Mill and Marx, Morris, Luxemburg, Orwell, and Russell—would have been somehow better off for having a proper metaphysical foundation for their aspirations. On the other hand, maybe the fact that they scraped along pretty well without one means that the question

"Why care about others?" and the larger question "Why act rightly?", which Taylor thinks can only be answered definitively by invoking some "constitutive good" can't be answered definitively at all. And needn't be.

Taylor is continually saying things like:

> To see the standard Enlightenment view as one- dimensional is to see no place in it for what makes life significant. Human life seems a matter merely of desire-fulfillment, but the very basis for strong evaluation, for there being desires or goals which are intrinsically worth fulfilling, seems missing.

It's clear that Taylor the man and citizen admires the ultra-naturalist *philosophes*, by and large, and considers their lives not just significant but exemplary. But for Taylor the philosopher, some "transcendental conditions" are apparently required to make a life "significant"; likewise to make desires and goals "intrinsically" worth fulfilling. It's not that the *philosophes* didn't have the right sort of desires and goals, just that they lacked an adequate "moral ontology," hence access to the "moral sources" and "constitutive goods" that would have allowed them to articulate the significance of their lives. They denied (or ought, on their own principles, to have denied) the reality of the virtues they practiced and the values they lived for.

Well, maybe so, but this contradiction doesn't seem to have slowed them down much. Taylor suggests that this is because the *philosophes*, and altruistic unbelievers ever since, have drawn spiritual sustenance from religious traditions, still potent in the eighteenth century though dwindling in influence today. But, he warns, this can't go on forever. No culture can permanently endure so basic a tension between its morality and its metaphysics (or antimetaphysics). "High standards need strong sources," he writes in the final pages of *Sources of the Self*.

> The question which arises from all this is whether or not we are living beyond our moral means in continuing allegiance to our standards of justice and benevolence. Do we have ways of

seeing-good which are still credible to us, which are powerful enough to sustain these standards? If not, it would be both more honest and more prudent to moderate them. . . . Is the naturalist seeing-good, which turns on the rejection of the calumny of religion against nature, fundamentally parasitic? This it might be in two senses: not only that it derives its affirmation through rejecting an alleged negation, but also that the original model for its universal benevolence is agape. How well could it survive the demise of the religion it strives to abolish? With the "calumny" gone, could the affirmation continue?

That is: perseverance in virtue will sometimes require self-sacrifice; and self-sacrifice seems to require some transcendental justification or motivation, of which the most common, and perhaps the most logical, is belief in the existence of God. Or so Taylor argues, circumspectly. Since modern freedom entails the rejection of transcendence, modern virtue is wholly contingent. Can we be good for long without God? Taylor's doubts are daunting.

And there lies the nerve of my discomfort: the suspicion, powerfully and plausibly albeit tactfully and tentatively expressed, that the ideals I most prize are at bottom inadequate. I confess I see no alternative to living with this suspicion, perhaps permanently.

But if it's not clear what, in the long run, best sustains commitments to justice and compassion, it's less difficult to see what, in the short run, precludes them (and most other fine and fruitful qualities as well): deprivation, insecurity, ideological manipulation. Is it too light-minded to suggest that even if altruism gives out, curiosity—the keenest of appetites, after all—might continue to motivate efforts to eliminate these evils? Just to see what humankind turns out to be like: just to see who was right, Taylor or Nietzsche or Condorcet?

Disciplines and Bondage

Michel Foucault, who died in June of 1984, was that rare phenomenon: a philosopher-superstar, a prophet honored in his own time. Except perhaps for Sartre, he was the most famous French thinker in an age that did not lack for distinguished—or at any rate celebrated—ones. Even during his (sadly foreshortened) life, he was often ranked with Freud, Wittgenstein, and Heidegger among the pre-eminent figures of the 20th century.

Foucault wrote one enormous history of the origins of psychiatry (published in English as *Madness and Civilization*), another of the origins of clinical medicine (*The Birth of the Clinic*), yet another of the origins of modern philology, biology, and political economy (*The Order of Things*), still another of the origins of prisons and penology (*Discipline and Punish*), and finally, another (multivolume and unfinished) of the vicissitudes of sexual theory and ideology (*The History of Sexuality*). He wrote a short, dense book explaining his methodology (*The Archaeology of Knowledge*) and many literary and philosophical essays. He was also a prolific interviewee. *A Foucault Reader** is the first anthology drawn from this large, idiosyncratic oeuvre, and it is hard to imagine a better one. No middle-sized anthology (and, a *fortiori*, no brief review) can hope to give an adequate account of Foucault's work, but the *Reader* places the emphasis where it ought to be: on his later, more political phase. And Paul Rabinow's introduction is excellent.

"History" is actually not quite the right word for what Foucault was up to. He himself labeled his activity "archaeology" (sometimes "genealogy," in homage to Nietzsche's *The Genealogy of Morals*). That is, he aimed to excavate the epistemological foundations of the "human sciences" (the French

*Edited by Paul Rabinow, Pantheon, 1984.

term *sciences de l'homme* includes psychology, linguistics, and cultural history as well as the social sciences). The historical development of these sciences may well seem, at first glance, to have been gradual and linear, a matter of continual growth and refinement, with a genetic relation between the problems and techniques of one age and those of the next. This seemingly natural view rests on and reinforces some deep assumptions: that the history of the sciences is a history of progress and that these disciplines are autonomous—i.e., that they have an intrinsic, not merely an instrumental, criterion of truth.

Foucault challenges these assumptions. His richly (though erratically) documented studies try to prove that new stages in the human sciences result not from the gradual transformation of preceding stages but from changes in the underlying "conditions of possibility" of knowledge in an era, a sort of epistemological deep structure that Foucault calls an episteme. "By episteme, we mean . . . the total set of relations that unite, at a given period, the discursive practices that give rise to epistemological figures, sciences, and formalizable systems . . . It is the totality of relations that can be discovered, for a given period, between the sciences when one analyzes them at the level of discursive regularities."

Foucault's early work, especially *The Order of Things,* is a staggeringly detailed yet dizzyingly abstract attempt to articulate these "discursive regularities." He divides up Western history since the Middle Ages into several broad epochs: the Renaissance, the Classical period (from the mid-17th century to the end of the 18th), the modern period (from the end of the 18th to the middle of the 20th century), and the postmodern period. Each is characterized by distinctive modes of representation, relations between signs and their objects, rules of inference and concept formation, and other subtle but profound differences in intellectual structure. For example, the 17th- and 18th-century predecessors of philology, biology, and economics were called, respectively, "general grammar," "natural history," and "the analysis of wealth." These three fields shared certain "rules of discourse," including the notion that all knowledge was classificatory in nature and could therefore be arranged in the form of a table. In the 19th century, however, the world was seen differently, as made up "not of isolated elements related by identity and difference, but of organic structures, of internal relations between elements whose totality performs a function."

Where these "rules of discourse" come from, whether they apply universally in each period, and what causes the shift from one epoch and its episteme to another are matters that Foucault never makes fully clear. This is the most obscure and controversial aspect of his work; even some of his admirers have begun to wonder out loud whether his "archaeology of knowledge" is not, finally, a magnificent dead end. It should be said, though, that for all their theoretical difficulty, *Madness and Civilization* and *The Birth of the Clinic* are full of fascinating detail and are, in their way, literary masterpieces. Watching Foucault read obscure treatises on the theory of fevers as rigorously and perceptively as some New Critics used to read lyric poetry, one can intuit the powers of the structuralist method, so often routinized or vulgarized by lesser thinkers.

Unlike the New Critics (and many structuralists), however, Foucault was always sensitive—at least implicitly—to the interplay of social change and intellectual change. Late in his career, he remarked in an interview: "I now ask myself what I was writing about in *Madness and Civilization* and *The Birth of the Clinic*, if not power?" What came between those books and that remark was the worker/student revolt of May 1968 in France. The protagonists of the "May events" sought to broaden the traditional scope of politics—to raise questions about the "politics of everyday life," about domination and liberation not only in factories but also in offices, schools, prisons, hospitals, families, and sexual relationships. The revolution failed, but its influence among French intellectuals, including Foucault, was vast. In the early 1970s, shortly after assuming a chair at the prestigious Collège de France, Foucault helped organize the

Groupe d'Information sur les Prisons, a prisoners'-rights group that played a part in winning some important reforms. That experience, and the new political atmosphere in which it took place, brought to the fore an issue that had hitherto been latent in his work but was to dominate it thereafter: the question of power.

Foucault's activity among prisoners led to *Discipline and Punish: the Birth of the Prison*, generally considered his best book and one of the premier works of social theory in recent decades. He asks: is it a coincidence that the word "discipline" means both "body of knowledge" and "technique of control"? By way of answer, he surveys the evolution of criminal punishment. Under the Ancien Régime, social order was conceived in terms of sovereignty. Like God, a monarch possessed unlimited power and was owed unlimited obedience. Crime was thus considered, at least in principle, a species of cosmic rebellion. Punishment was the reassertion of cosmic order: an infinitely legitimate and powerful sovereign would publicly impose infinitely painful punishment, which simultaneously reassured and intimidated the populace. Punishment was theater, and as a result, criminal justice under the Ancien Régime was harsh but sporadic.

This cruelty and irregularity were among the prime targets of Enlightenment reformers. Like liberal reformers in every age, they argued that a more "rational" (i.e., methodical) approach would prove both more humane and more effective. The genius of *Discipline and Punish* lies in showing how "effective" swallowed "humane." "The true objective of the reform movement . . . was not so much to establish a new right to punish based on more equitable principles, as to set up a new 'economy' of the power to punish, to assure its better distribution, so that it should be . . . capable of operating everywhere, in a continuous way, down to the finest grain of the social body."

Social "science" came into being as a means of social control. The reformers claimed that more effective criminal justice required better knowledge—first of all about criminals, and then about the population and environment from which they had emerged. Knowledge about criminals meant isolating and observing them; hence the birth of the prison. But knowledge of the population meant something much grander and more ominous; a whole "disciplinary technology" of statistics, case histories, surveillance, training—in short, the sciences of administration. *Discipline and Punish* might well have been subtitled *The Birth of Bureaucracy*.

The implications of this new "disciplinary technology" are incalculable. In a way, Foucault suggests, it has altered the very nature of individuality:

> For a long time ordinary individuality—the everyday individuality of everybody—remained below the threshold of description. To be looked at, observed, described in detail, followed from day to day by an uninterrupted writing, was a privilege. The chronicle of a man, the account of his life, his historiography, written as he lived out his life, formed part of the rituals of his power. The disciplinary methods reversed this relation, lowered the threshold of describable individuality and made of this description a means of control and a method of domination. It is no longer a monument for future memory, but a document for possible use . . . The turning of real lives into writing is no longer a procedure of hero-ization; it functions as a procedure of objectification and subjection.

The equation of "writing" with "objectification" (developed in detail in *Discipline and Punish*) is one of those dazzling imaginative leaps that make Foucault's work well worth its many difficulties.

Here is another, from his discussion of Jeremy Bentham's notorious "Panopticon," an architectural plan meant to permit total surveillance in prisons, hospitals, schools, factories, and barracks:

> Bentham was the complement to Rousseau. What in fact was the Rousseauist dream that motivated many of the [18th-century] revolutionaries? It was the dream of a transparent society, visible and legible in each of its parts; the dream of there no longer existing any zones of darkness, zones established by the

privileges of royal power or the prerogatives of some corpora-
tion, zones of disorder. It was the dream that each individual,
whatever position he occupied, might be able to see the whole
of society, that men's hearts should communicate, their vision
be unobstructed by obstacles, and that the opinion of all reign
over each . . . This reign of "opinion," so often invoked at the
time, represents a mode of operation through which power will
be exercised by virtue of the mere fact of things being known
and people seen in a sort of immediate, collective, and anon-
ymous gaze. A form of power whose main instance is that of
opinion will refuse to tolerate areas of darkness.

This description of the "transparent society" can be read, with
20th-century hindsight, as a genealogy of totalitarianism.
When one reflects on the root of the term Enlightenment, the
irony is unbearable. In passages like these, Foucault approaches
Nietzsche and Weber in stature, as one of the greatest critics of
modernity.

Foucault's last project was the unfinished *History of Sexuality*. It is, once again, not a history; and it is not primarily about
sex. It is about power—more precisely, about the intimate association between power and knowledge. The conventional wisdom (Foucault calls it "the repressive hypothesis") holds that
the "natural" sexuality of rural societies was repressed in the
interest of the capitalist work ethic. The 19th-century bour-
geoisie, especially, imposed silence and shamefulness upon
sex. In this view, sex is a mute, biologically given, potentially
subversive force awaiting its liberation by a true, unashamed
discourse, such as psychoanalysis once gave promise of being.

Foucault argues that, on the contrary, no epoch was more
voluble about sex than the 19th century. The period witnessed
an avalanche of theories about female, child, and "deviant"
sexuality. Among the notions invented and elaborated in this
period: the concept of chronic female hysteria; a campaign
against childhood masturbation; the medicalization of homo-
sexuality and other non-procreative sexual behavior; and the
first systematic social policies regarding population, birth control, and sexual hygiene. The purpose of all this discourse was

not, however, the liberation of sexuality; it was the rationalization, the "normalization," of sexuality. Sexual "science," like the rest of the social sciences, originated as a mode of social control, as an aspect of "disciplinary technology."

"Rationalization"—that profoundly ambiguous word—is in fact one way to sum up Foucault's lifelong theme. He once proposed this definition of the "central issue" in modern thought: "What is this Reason that we use? What are its historical effects? What are its limits, and what are its dangers? How can we exist as rational beings, fortunately committed to practicing a rationality that is unfortunately crisscrossed by intrinsic dangers?" No one who has pondered Foucault's epic investigations will ever again be quite without ambivalence about "this Reason that we use."

But does all this relentless demystification of progress, of science, of Reason itself, leave room for any hope of our ultimate emancipation? To have exposed the penetration of disciplinary bureaucratic power down to "the finest grain of the social body" is an invaluable achievement. But if that power is truly ubiquitous, if it's constitutive of our very individuality, as Foucault suggests, then how can we escape it? If power relations are universal, then there is no trans-historical Reason or truth or human nature. And if we can appeal to no such transcendental standard, how can we ever transcend power relations?

Foucault never answered that question. He might have tried, if he'd lived longer (or he might not). The closest he came was an occasional ambiguous pronouncement like this:

> The political, ethical, social, philosophical problem of our days is not to try to liberate the individual from the state, and from the state's institutions, but to liberate us from both the state and the type of individualization which is linked to the state. We have to promote new forms of subjectivity through the refusal of the kind of individuality which has been imposed on us for several centuries.

The mind reels at the difficulty of interpreting, much less implementing, this program.

There's no gainsaying that Foucault was a negative thinker: his rigorous determinism can make B. F. Skinner seem almost Pollyanna-ish, and his infrequent radical affirmations are, as often as not, half-hearted, provisional, ironic. But the energy and subtlety of his negativism is itself a precious resource. Whatever the shape of our liberation may finally be, we now know a good deal more, thanks to Foucault, about the many shapes of domination.

A Representative Destiny

Henry James aspired to be "one of those on whom nothing is lost." It is, even in principle, an impossible aspiration. Beyond a certain point, depth and breadth, originality and comprehensiveness, are inversely related. This is the fact of finitude, the root of tragedy: that to see deeply into anything, one must be blind to a great deal. Unlimited receptivity, perfect negative capability, may in the end be disabling, even for an artist. James is himself a poignant example.

A very few writers have, however, attained something like James's ideal, none more so than Nietzsche. In his intellectual testament, *Ecce Homo,* Nietzsche described his work as "a critique of modernity." Every important strain in 19th-century European culture—classical antiquity, Christianity, the Enlightenment, German idealism, Romanticism, science, socialism, feminism, even Orientalism—played an essential part in that critique. Of course Nietzsche did not do impartial justice to each of these; more often, sublime injustice. He could, after all, hardly afford even the pretence of impartiality. Others—Aristotle, Aquinas, Leibniz, Hegel—had likewise mastered nearly every aspect of contemporary thought and achieved a kind of synthesis. But each of these was more or less in harmony with his age. Nietzsche was in radical opposition to his. He was at once the foremost interpreter and the foremost antagonist of his—our—civilization. His encounter with modernity was a war; the record of that war was an epic; the hero of that epic was Nietzsche.

A hero of consciousness, a "representative destiny" (Karl Jaspers): this is how Nietzsche has appeared in every subsequent generation. But the terms of his influence have altered. The first form of that influence was the image of Nietzsche the prophet, the diagnostician of nihilism and herald of its overcoming. Nietzsche was perhaps not the first to recognize that everything previously held capable of giving meaning to history—in a word, "God"—could no longer be believed in. But he perceived the consequences of that fact with unprecedented clarity and faced up to them with unprecedented seriousness. In the most advanced ideologies of his time—egalitarianism, positivism, nationalism—he claimed to see just so many attempts to evade those consequences, to retain the metaphysical and moral superstitions that only the freest spirits could do without. Nietzsche proposed to teach, not through a doctrine but by his example, how to live without illusions—how to live under the volcano. And to live well:

> He who, prompted by some enigmatic desire, has, like me, long endeavored to think pessimism through to the bottom . . . he who has really gazed with an Asiatic and more than Asiatic eye down into the most world-denying of all possible modes of thought—beyond good and evil and no longer, like Buddha and Schopenhauer, under the spell and illusion of morality—perhaps by that very act, and without really seeking to, may have had his eyes opened to the opposite ideal: to the ideal of the most exuberant, most living, and most world-affirming man, who has not only learned to get on and treat with all that was and is but who wants to have it again as it was and is to all eternity, insatiably crying out da capo not only to himself but to the whole piece and play. . . .

Nothing lost, nothing negated: the ideal of the "superman."

This is the Nietzsche that Thomas Mann called "a personality of phenomenal cultural plenitude and complexity, summing up all that is essentially European"; that looms in the immediate background of Freud, Rilke, Gide, Shaw, and Lawrence; and that others carelessly mistook for, or cynically distorted into, a proto-Nazi. But since Nietzsche's time, the center of gravity of Western thought has shifted from history to language, from *Kulturkritik* to structuralism. For better or worse, Nietzsche the prophet is out of fashion today, while Nietzsche the philosopher has come into his own. To put this distinction another way: Nietzsche the psychologist, the "immoralist," the

Antichrist, seems less interesting to most contemporary philosophers and literary critics than Nietzsche the epistemologist, the theorist of knowledge and language. As one of his contemporary interpreters has written, Nietzsche, like his postmodern successors, "teaches us not how to live but how to read."

The latter, formalist mode is less obviously heroic than the earlier, world-historical one. But nihilism has its epistemological form, which must also be overcome. To show how Nietzsche accomplished this, and in doing so to trace the deep structure of modernity's various nihilisms and Nietzsche's various heroisms, is the aim of Alexander Nehamas's *Nietzsche: Life as Literature**.

Nehamas begins by posing an apparently peripheral question: why does Nietzsche write aphoristically, hyperbolically, and in such a variety of genres? Most of Nietzsche's readers probably assume that this is an accident of temperament or else a symbolic rejection of order and coherence, which do not, Nietzsche claims, characterize the world and therefore should not characterize philosophical writing. But there is more to it than that. In the course of answering his initial question Nehamas evolves a wonderfully subtle and ingenious interpretation, one that hints at Nietzsche's almost unrivalled capacity to teach us "how to live" as well as "how to read."

Consider the reactions that Nietzsche's hyperbole typically produces: a defensive indifference, which claims that nothing serious and philosophical could possibly be said in such a style; active indignation and hostility; or uncritical discipleship. This is the same range of reactions evoked by Nietzsche's antipodes and lifelong antagonist, Socrates; and not accidentally, since both were intensely personal thinkers, with designs upon the lives of their readers/listeners. But Socrates' characteristic trope is litotes: ironic, self-effacing understatement. Socrates' style tends to make him, as an "author," invisible; Nietzsche's makes him insistently visible. The reason for this antithesis is

*Harvard University Press, 1986.

that Socrates introduced theory into ethics. He was the first to claim that reasoning could produce moral judgments of impersonal, universal validity—"dogmas" in the ancient, non-pejorative sense. This seemed to Nietzsche the most fateful and disastrous innovation in the history of thought, and he devoted his whole career to showing that pretensions to objective moral truth, i.e., to dogma, invariably mask that most personal of motives, the will to power. One of his tactics in this struggle was to develop a style that, in direct opposition to that of Socrates, was so personal and figurative as to be virtually incapable of syllogistic paraphrase. Nietzsche's fundamental proposition, his "perspectivism," holds that all theories and values are individual perspectives and that the world, like a work of literature, can be interpreted equally well in different, even incompatible ways. His style enacts that proposition.

Nietzsche's perspectivism rests on his critique of the metaphysics of identity. Traditionally, most philosophers believed in an abstract and universal human nature, which gave to each human being an immutable identity. This identity, or self, underlay the individual's diverse attributes and actions. In one form or another, this distinction between the universal and the individual, the self and its attributes, has appeared throughout the history of philosophy: spirit and matter, essence and accident, substance and property, soul and body, reality and appearance, thing-in-itself and phenomenon. And everywhere it appeared, belief in a universal human nature has been the basis of belief in a universal human morality, valid unconditionally, at all times and places, for all human beings.

That belief had been under attack since 14th-century nominalism. The radical phenomenalism of Hume, revised by Kant, had weakened it gravely. Nietzsche undertook to deliver the *coup de grace* and to produce new answers, not dependent on metaphysical fictions, to the perennial questions: what is "truth"? what is a "self"? what is the "good"?

Nietzsche approached these questions by trying to dissolve the categorical distinctions that had, in each case, structured the traditional answers. In the case of truth, these were "fact" vs. "interpretation," "objective" vs. "subjective," and most obviously, "true" vs. "false." Nietzsche argued that there are no simple "facts," i.e. that the world has no features that are prior to and independent of every interpretation (a view now fairly standard among philosophers of science); that every interpretation is crucially influenced by the goals and temperaments of those who devise it; and that every general theory must involve sweeping simplifications and logical compromises or else sacrifice comprehensibility and relevance to ordinary life.

As for the "self," Nietzsche showed that "intellect" and "will" are not separate faculties, which somehow exist apart from thoughts and volitions. What's more, thoughts, volitions, and emotions are themselves complex, continuous processes, indissoluble from their objects and effects. So much, then, for the "soul" and for metaphysical personhood; a self is a set of interconnections grouped together by an interpretation. Or, in one of Nietzsche 's countless arresting phrases, "a 'thing' is the sum of its effects."

Most famously, Nietzsche argued that judgments about "good" and "evil," like all other valuations, are historical through and through. In a sense roughly comparable to Marx's critique of ideology, Nietzsche claimed that a morality is one group's preferred way of life masquerading as an obligatory way of life for all groups. He even wrote the history of one successful masquerade: his "genealogy" of Christian morals, which aimed to show how the underclass of the ancient world had rationalized its submission into a morality of submissiveness.

If one accepts this stringent reductionism, then our familiar conceptual landscape, with its handy signposts like "thing," "mind," and "virtue," is no longer recognizable. The world as Nietzsche describes it would seem to be a place of complete epistemological and moral fluidity, containing nothing absolute or unequivocal. It is as though, to paraphrase Dostoevsky, if metaphysics does not exist, everything is permitted, in discourse as well as deed.

But it is not at all clear how we could live in, or even make sense of, such a world. And so Nietzsche has been suspected of paradox. If every general view is no more than an interpretation, the expression of an individual perspective, then what is the status of this view itself—is it "true"? How, precisely, can there be actions without agents, effects without things? And how can Nietzsche criticize existing morality except, at least implicitly, in virtue of some positive morality of his own, which would then, by his own argument, be as arbitrary and dogmatic as those he is criticizing? Doesn't Nietzsche's methodological reductionism undermine itself?

Nehamas shows that it does not, provided we recognize that Nietzsche conceived of the world as formally equivalent to a work of literature, of interpretation as literary criticism, and of persons as literary characters. Nietzsche's "negative" achievement was to demonstrate that the world could not be understood metaphysically. His "positive" achievement was to demonstrate that it could be understood aesthetically. His solutions to the traditional problems of philosophy became intelligible if we rephrase those problems in this way: What is a "true" or "correct" interpretation of a work of art? What is the "identity" of a literary character? What makes a character "good" or admirable? Nehamas answers:

> If persons do not have natures and things do not have essences, then the world does not have a single, uniquely real, "ontological" structure that underlies mere appearances. That is, the world is indeterminate. Just as the complete family tree of any person would include every other person who has ever lived, the complete causal history of any event would include everything that has ever happened. Every person has an infinite number of possible family trees and every event has an infinite number of possible causes. Which family history or causal sequence is "correct" depends on our purposes in asking for it.

How, then, does Nietzsche imagine that we construct usable definitions and explanations? By composing narratives. "The unity of each thing, that thing itself, is to be found in the genealogical account that connects one set of phenomena to another. It is to be found in a narrative of the way in which the later set can be seen as the descendant—not as a development, manifestation, or appearance—of the set that came earlier. Genealogy is Nietzsche's alternative to ontology."

A genealogical narrative is fictive, constructed; it does not pretend to reflect the ultimate nature of things, since there isn't one. Its success, like that of literary criticism, depends on revealing the maximum number of interconnections in a text or situation with a minimum of forcing. This, according to Nietzsche, is true of interpretations generally.

It is also true of lives. In *The Gay Science* Nietzsche writes:

> *One thing is needful.*—To "give style" to one's character—a great and rare art! It is practiced by all those who survey the strengths and weaknesses of their nature and then fit them into an artistic plan until every one of them appears as art and reason and even weaknesses delight the eye. . . . In the end, when the work is finished, it becomes evident how the constraint of a single taste governed and formed everything large and small. Whether this taste was good or bad is less important than one might suppose, if only it was a single taste!

Here is Nehamas' gloss: "A person consists of absolutely everything he or she thinks, wants, and does. But a person worthy of admiration, a person who has (or is) a self, is one whose thoughts, desires, and actions are not haphazard but are instead connected to one another in the intimate way that indicates in all cases the presence of style. A self is just a set of coherently connected episodes, and an admirable self, as Nietzsche insists again and again, consists of a large number of powerful and conflicting tendencies that are controlled and harmonized. Coherence, of course, can also be produced by weakness and one-dimensionality. But style, which is what Nietzsche requires and admires, involves controlled multiplicity and resolved conflict."

In other words, exactly the same qualities that make an interpretation successful—breadth, consistency, piquancy, richness of texture—make a character admirable. Just as the world has no ontological structure that makes a single type of interpretation "true," it has no moral structure that makes a single type of character "good." Instead, Nietzsche's model for the world is the self-contained unity of a work of literature. There are "good" (well-constructed) and "bad" (poorly constructed) characters in fiction, but they are not for that reason "good" or "evil."

"Style" is, however, a purely formal criterion. Does Nietzsche really mean to praise, say, Richard III equally with his beloved Goethe just because both personalities were the work of "a single taste"? Can't he affirm any specific moral qualities, or is that disallowed by his perspectivism? Nehamas's answer is equivocal. Nietzsche "thinks that admirable people are one and all what he calls 'individuals.' But the very notion of an individual is one that essentially refuses to be spelled out in informative terms. To give general directions for becoming an individual is surely as self-defeating as is offering general views when one believes that general views are all simply interpretations." Or, one may add, as futile as offering general directions for creating a work of art.

Nietzsche could not, without self-contradiction, theorize about his ideal way of life; that would have been to fall back into the dogmatism of Socrates and the rest of the philosophical tradition. But he could not simply abandon philosophy for literature without leaving that dogmatism intact. His solution to this dilemma was to embody his philosophical views in a character, whom he implicitly commends to his readers. This character strove for and attained "style" in Nietzsche's sense by fashioning an extraordinary multiplicity of materials—literary forms, dictions, subject matters—into a complex, idiosyncratic unity. He illustrated Nietzsche's *amor fati,* or fatalism, by accepting and turning to his own advantage such grievous misfortunes as wretched health, a mistaken early choice of career, and an equally mistaken early choice of mentor. And he placed himself beyond good and evil by becoming deeply admirable—or at least widely admired—in the very process of repudiating every morality known to him.

"Nietzsche's texts do not describe but, in exquisitely elaborate detail, *exemplify* the perfect instance of his ideal character. And this character is none other than the character these very texts constitute: Nietzsche himself." This character, "Nietzsche," is not the sickly, lonely, high-strung man who wrote Nietzsche's works, but the fascinating and terrible voice that speaks them. Nietzsche's "Nietzsche" is like Plato's Socrates, a supremely influential figure who is also a fictional creation—only in Nietzsche's case, self-consciously so.

This account scarcely begins to suggest the subtlety and rigor of Nehamas's interpretation. *Nietzsche: Life as Literature* is about as good as academic philosophy gets. Still, the radical formalism of Nehamas's approach has its disadvantages. For one thing, it risks leaving the impression that Nietzsche was tremendously, but merely, clever. Karl Jaspers observed that Nietzsche "did not so much think his problems as suffer them." Of course no interpretation can reproduce the incomparable pathos of Nietzsche's writing. But the spareness and dispassion of Nehamas's prose makes for an especially sharp, sometimes frustrating contrast with the abundance and vivacity of Nietzsche's. Although this is hardly Nehamas's fault, it seems worth pointing out, if only to remind readers that Nietzsche was a great artist as well as a great philosopher.

He was also—there's no ignoring it—a prophet. I don't mean this in the customary sense, which tends to highlight such predictions as "For when truth enters into a fight with the lies of millennia, we shall have upheavals, a convulsion of earthquakes, a moving of mountains and valleys, the like of which has never been dreamed of. The concept of politics will have merged entirely with a war of spirits; all power structures of the old society will have been exploded—all of them are based on lies: there will be wars the like of which have never yet been seen on earth. It is only beginning with me that the earth knows *great politics*." This Nietzsche is, perhaps understandably, neglected nowadays. I mean the Nietzsche about whom Freud said that "he had a more penetrating knowledge of himself than any other man who ever lived or was likely to live" and that "his premonitions and insights often agree in the most amazing manner with the laborious results of psychoanalysis."

To me (and also, I would guess, to Nehamas), the summit of Nietzsche's achievement is the essay on asceticism in *The Genealogy of Morals.* There are several fine pages on this essay in *Nietzsche: Life as Literature,* which say virtually everything important about it—except that its central enigma has since received an answer, or the outlines of an answer. Nietzsche argues that the apparently life-denying ascetic ideal is actually life-preserving, since the guilt it invents as an explanation for human suffering shields people from the unbearable recognition that suffering has no explanation. But some of the language in which Nietzsche describes asceticism suggests that a part of this seemingly inexorable suffering may have an explanation after all, though one that was not available to Nietzsche. The ascetic spirit, he writes, "springs from the protective instinct of a degenerating life." The victim knows that he is "suffering from himself in some way or other," and senses obscurely that he must seek the cause "in a piece of the past; he must understand his suffering as a *punishment.*" But unable either to exorcize or to ignore this "piece of the past," he tries to "deaden, by means of a more violent emotion of any kind, a tormenting, secret pain that is becoming unendurable, and to drive it out of consciousness at least for a moment." At its most extreme, this deadening turns into a fantasy of annihilation: "this horror of the senses, of reason itself, this fear of happiness and beauty, this longing to get away from all appearance, change, becoming, death, wishing, from longing itself—all this means—let us dare grasp it—*a will to nothingness.*" Nietzsche's portrait of the sick soul anticipates "in the most amazing manner" one of those "laborious results of psychoanalysis": the theory of pathological narcissism, which charts the transformation of "a piece of the past"—infantile rage and terror—into something uncannily like the "deadening" Nietzsche describes. And there is another striking premonition in one of his phrases about the ascetic ideal: "life wrestles in it and through it with death and *against* death." *Life Against Death*, perhaps the most original and fruitful interpretation of Freud, is deeply indebted to *The Genealogy of Morals* and is, in a sense, also an essay on asceticism.

Nehamas does not do entire justice to Nietzsche the psychologist. But then, every perspective must leave something out. *Nietzsche: Life as Literature* is, along with R. J. Hollingdale's superb *Nietzsche* (1973)*, the best study in English. Fittingly, given its subject, it illustrates the continuity between making interpretations and making art. Of "Nietzsche," Nehamas writes:

> This character does not provide a model for imitation, since he consists essentially of the specific actions—that is, of the specific writings—that make him up, and which only he could write. To imitate him directly would produce a caricature, or at best a copy—something which in either case is not an individual. To imitate him properly would produce a creation which, making use of everything that properly belongs to oneself, would also be perfectly one's own—something which is no longer an imitation.

Nehamas has imitated "Nietzsche" properly. He has produced something weighty, complex, distinctive—in its way, a work of art. Not, like Niezsche's, a masterwork, but unquestionably something with "style."

*Routledge, 1973.

The Wages of Original Sin

"Isn't it curious," my theology teacher used to say with a sly smile, "that beyond good and evil is always . . . evil?" This is traditionally the last resort, the trump card, of the orthodox: that there is no honor among unbelievers, or at least no security for their honor. Why should someone who doesn't love God, or at least fear His judgment, be moral? In *God Is Not Great*, Christopher Hitchens recalls a debate between the philosopher A. J. Ayer and an Anglican bishop about the existence of God. Apparently out of arguments, the bishop exclaimed: "But if you really believe all that, why don't you immediately go out and commit every sort of depraved act?" It hadn't occurred to His Grace that a skeptic, even a skeptical Oxford philosopher, could be anything but wicked.

Contemporary social science has pretty well established that believers and unbelievers commit every sort of depraved act in roughly equal proportions. Nevertheless, the assumption that one cannot be reliably good without God persists in the United States, explicitly or implicitly, to the extent that a declared unbeliever almost certainly cannot be elected to national office. Around half the population identify themselves as born-again Christians and believe in angels, miracles, the inerrancy of the Bible, and the special creation of the Earth within the last ten thousand years. So if (as everyone seems to agree) America is in decline morally, an excess of skeptical rationalism is probably not to blame. Still, the modern world is undeniably more secular than the pre-modern one, especially among the educated, and that fact must surely have large psychological, if not behavioral, consequences. What have been, and will be, the effects of the Enlightenment on the individual and collective moral psychology of the West?

For five decades, until his death in July 2006, Philip Rieff pondered that question intently, learnedly, and eccentrically. Though Rieff was a sociology professor, he was not a social scientist; he was a social theorist in the line of Durkheim and Weber, an erudite synthesizer. All three were social psychologists of religion, but Rieff was a social psychologist of irreligion as well. Equally important, he had an analytical resource they did not: Freudian psychoanalysis.

Rieff's first book (his best, in my opinion) was a penetrating and imaginative study, *Freud: The Mind of the Moralist* (1959). At the time, most people considered Freud an immoralist—a proponent of liberation. Morality was supposedly what made us ill, posing unreasonable demands on behalf of "civilization" and forcing our healthy instinctual passions underground, into the unconscious, from which they tried to escape by way of "symptoms." These symptoms were strangled protests against the tyranny of culture over nature. The psychoanalytic cure was a protracted guerrilla campaign, aiming to take over one inner stronghold after another without provoking an all-out counterattack in the form of a nervous breakdown.

Freudian therapy was an indifferent success, but Freudian theory was enormously influential. The lesson most people took from it was a strong suspicion of moral authority and a reluctance to exercise it over young children. Inhibition, repression, and conformity were assumed to be unhealthy; spontaneity, individualism, and self-expression to be healthy. The prestige of "order" plummeted; that of "freedom" soared.

The Mind of the Moralist was a vigorous dissent from this standard interpretation. Rieff's point was not just that, unlike his noisier disciples, Freud was temperamentally conservative, rating order as highly as freedom and restraint as highly as expression. This stance could be (and regularly was) dismissed as reflexive Victorian/Viennese caution. On the contrary, Rieff argued, Freud's caution was well-founded. He understood that he had not really explained away our primal, nameless sense of guilt, which lay beneath the more superficial and intelligible constraints imposed by culture, with the implausible hypothesis of a primal crime. And yet, for this resolute unbeliever, such guilt could have no rational basis—who, after all, was humankind accountable to?

Rieff's explanation of what there is to be guilty about has been repeated in many books over many years, with increasing urgency (and, it must be said, portentousness). Human possibilities are limitless; about this he seemed to agree with Freud's liberationist successors. But what excited them terrified him—and likewise, he claimed, everyone else before the triumph of the therapeutic ethos. Our primal endowment—formless, destructive, uncontrollable instinct—paralyzes and isolates us. We cannot trust ourselves or one another until a firm structure of interdictions has been installed in everyone's psyche. These must be expounded by an interpretive elite, ratified through a calendar of rituals, and enforced by stern authority. Every culture is a dialectic of prohibition and permission, renunciation and release. Freud would have agreed; but whereas his followers concluded that the original "yes" of instinct was silenced, or at least muted, by the "no" of repressive authority, Rieff countered that instinct was cacophonous and only the original, creative "no" gave it a distinct voice. As he put it in *The Mind of the Moralist*—his style, already a little melodramatic, foreshadowing his later, full-blown apocalyptic abstractions—the primal self is "in a panic to express the fecundity of its own emptiness" and must be mastered by "unalterable authority." For if "everything could be expressed by everyone identically," then "nothing would remain to be expressed individually." Hence the "irreducible and supreme activity of culture" is to "prevent the expression of everything," thereby precluding "the one truly egalitarian dominion: nothingness."

For most educated (even many uneducated) Westerners, however, all formerly unalterable authorities now lie in the dust, like Ozymandias. Science has banished the supernatural, technology has vanquished scarcity; and so, having lost its parents, ignorance and misery, morality is now an orphan. This is the triumphalist view of modernity. Rieff agreed about the story line; only instead of a triumph, he thought it a catastrophe. The dimensions of this catastrophe dawned on him gradually. The last chapter of *Freud* is "The Emergence of Psychological Man," a tentative sketch of what modernity had wrought. Until the twentieth century, in Rieff's account, three character types had successively prevailed in Western culture: political man, the ideal of classical times, dedicated to the glory of his city; religious man, the ideal of the Christian era, dedicated to the glory of God; and a transitional figure, economic man, a creature of Enlightenment liberalism. Economic man believed in doing good unto others by doing well for himself. This convenient compromise did not last long, and what survived of it was not the altruism but the egoism. Psychological man was frankly and shrewdly selfish, beyond ideals and illusions, a charming narcissist at best, at worst boorish or hypochondriacal, according to his temperament.

But the worst thing about psychological man was his children. Raised without repressions, they were incapable of renunciation and regarded all authority as illegitimate. Rieff's second book, *The Triumph of the Therapeutic* (1966), raised the alarm about their "devastating illusions of individuality and freedom." A society without hierarchy, whose members "cannot conceive any salvation other than amplitude in living itself," must end in moral squalor, chaos, anomie, and universal boredom. Nor will it help to "disguise their rancorous worship of self in the religion of art," for art too depends on renunciation. Here Rieff quotes Nietzsche at length (in what is for me the most illuminating passage in Rieff's entire corpus):

> Every system of morals is a sort of tyranny against "nature" and also against "reason"; that is, however, no objection, unless one should decree, by some other system of morals, that all kinds of tyranny and unreasonableness are unlawful. What is essential and invaluable in every system of morals is that it is a long constraint. . . . The singular fact remains that everything of the nature of freedom, elegance, boldness, dance, and masterly certainty, which exists or has ever existed, whether in thought or administration, in art or in conduct, has only developed by

means of the tyranny of such arbitrary law; and in all seriousness, it is not at all improbable that precisely this is "nature" and
"natural" and not *laisser-aller*! . . . The essential thing is apparently (to repeat it once more) that there should be long obedience in the same direction; thereby results, and has always
resulted in the long run, something which has made life worth
living. (*Beyond Good and Evil*, #188)

Muscular strength is built gradually, for example by overcoming the resistance of progressively heavier weights. Moral
and psychological strength also require resistance—the pressure of cultural interdicts, dictating what is not to be done or
even thought of. Such discipline simplifies our lives and econo-
mizes our energies. Without an unquestioned moral demand
system, based on guilt, fear, and faith and generating obedience, trust, and dependence, there can be no spiritual hygiene,
no communal purpose. And that is what the triumph of the
therapeutic ethos makes impossible. Nowadays "the religious
psychologies of release and the social technologies of affluence
do not go beyond release and affluence to a fresh imposition of
restrictive demands. This describes, in a sentence, the cultural
revolution of our time. The old culture of denial has become
irrelevant to a world of infinite abundance and reality." In the
absence of strict, even harsh, limits (to use a plain word Rieff
himself so seldom used that one is led to wonder whether his
elaborately artificial prose style was itself meant as a discipline),
we cannot thrive.

While Rieff was writing *The Triumph of the Therapeutic*
in the early 1960s, the New Left and the counterculture were
still gathering force. When the storm broke in the mid- and
late sixties, he was aghast. In 1971 he gave an interview to the
editors of *Salmagundi*. When they asked him to edit the tran-
script for publication, he responded with a book-length open
letter, *Fellow Teachers* (1973), denouncing students and teachers alike, the former for their ignorant impatience of all discipline and sacred authority, the latter for their irresponsible
acquiescence.

Students can bring us no hope at all until the protest style, as Love of Humanity and Power to the People, is seen through. With the vision of this horror, we will see in true light the craven aping and interminable apologies for the transgressive types at the bottom: the perverts, the underclass, all those who can do no wrong because they have been wronged. . . . I repeat what I have said often: immediately behind the hippies are the thugs. They occupy the remissive space opened up by the hippies, deepening it from an aesthetic into a politics. The self-absorbed therapy of the hippies clears the way for the mass-murder therapy of the thugs.

He could not refrain from the ultimate epithet: "Released from sacred fear by our remissive teaching elites, transgressives carry their peculiar authority with more right and less shame than ever before in the history of our misery. Hitler and Holocaust . . . . Gulag and Dachau, torture and terror, are the dry-eyed children of our enlightenments."

Despairing, Rieff fell silent until his death thirty-three years later. (One of his students, Jonathan Imber, published *The Feeling Intellect*, a valuable collection of Rieff's occasional writings, in 1990.) He did not, however, cease working. He left behind a mass of manuscripts, which several former students were helping him ready for publication. One of them, *My Life Among the Deathworks*, appeared last year. The remaining manuscripts make up a trilogy, *Sacred Order, Social Order*, of which *Charisma** is the first volume.

Charisma is not Rieff at his best. The proofreading is slapdash; he would have been mortified by the quantity of faulty punctuation remaining. But he is also at fault: the book is repetitive, dense with jargon, impatient of exposition, and more than occasionally intemperate. In form, it is an extended quarrel with Max Weber's sociology of religion, which relies on the concept of charisma but, according to Rieff, radically misunderstands it. Weber conceived charisma as one of three kinds of authority—traditional, charismatic, and bureaucratic—that characterize

*Pantheon, 2007.

all organizations, including religious ones. Traditional authority, typical of primitive societies, derives from inertia and aims at continuity. Bureaucratic authority, typical of modern societies, derives from methodical reasoning and aims at efficiency. Charismatic authority is untypical and unpredictable; it derives from a singularly compelling, dynamic figure, seemingly gifted by God, and aims at radical reform or innovation. The charismatic figure arises when a tradition or bureaucracy stagnates, and his legacy is inevitably regularized by his uncharismatic successors. Since Weber, the term has been drastically vulgarized and is now mostly employed by journalists or publicists to puff politicians and pop-culture personalities.

Rieff deplores this progressive secularization of charisma and insists on its fundamentally religious significance. "My position is . . . no charisma without creed." For Rieff, a creed is not primarily theological but moral: a "particular order of interdicts and remissions." Genuine charisma is not transgressive; it does not abolish limits or license lawlessness. Rather, it imposes new interdicts, a "new organization of avoidances and of salvation through avoidances." Charismatics satisfy "the need for love in its prototypical form, as a craving for authority, reorganizing its expression within a fresh content of ambivalences." As he writes, in one of all too many suggestive but obscure passages:

> The suffering that is the predicate for a charismatic situation is therefore not material suffering as such, but the deprivation of that authority that is inseparable from the love relation. The revolutionary authority of the charismatic is not a cure when viewed from the perspective of a therapeutically sophisticated culture, but rather, another symptom of the prototypal series with the resistances reorganized to express yet different repressions.

Besides Weber, Rieff engages with the Old Testament prophets, Saint Paul, and Kierkegaard. His exegeses are ingenious and original, and they all yield the same conclusion: religion is prohibition, culture is inhibition, authority is salvation, submission is wisdom, transgression is folly, and criticism of anything but the pretensions of critical reason is impiety. Modern American society has so completely forgotten these lessons that one is constantly expecting to hear Rieff exclaim, like Heidegger, "Only a God can save us."

In all his books—indeed, on virtually every page—Rieff propounded a single thesis: the urgent necessity of a "sacred order," promulgated by a "creedal organization," consisting of "interdicts and remissions," admitting of no appeal and no criticism—except, if it should decay, from prophets who either purify and reaffirm the old interdictory order or establish a new one. Without this, he warned continually, no greatness of soul, no lasting happiness, no common life is possible.

And yet Rieff never—not once—suggested what the basis of a plausible sacred order might be. The old faiths, he acknowledged, have lost their hold on Western elites; but he offered no hint, scarcely even any hope, of a new one. It is as though a prophet came among the people, foretold a terrible future, and admonished: "You must believe and obey, or you are lost." And when the people cried out in earnest: "We cannot abide that future; tell us, then, what to believe and whom to obey," he replied: "It matters not what or whom; only believe and obey."

Prescribing religion without specifying any particular theology has become commonplace among social critics, particularly communitarians. One can understand why. No society—for that matter, no individual—can flourish without a great deal of trust, devotion, solidarity, and self-discipline. Religion often fosters these things, and not only among co-religionists. But although untrammeled sexual freedom is not a requirement of human flourishing, any more than the untrammeled freedom to accumulate money, untrammeled intellectual freedom most certainly is. Unquestioned authority is not merely undesirable, it is impossible, a contradiction in terms. Authority is what remains after all questions have been asked, all objections posed, all doubts explored. Until then, there is only superstition or cowed silence. Religious orthodoxy, and in particular the theistic hypothesis, has had many centuries to establish its intellectual authority. Its prospects are dwindling. If trust, devotion, and the other requisites of community depend on a general belief in supernatural agencies, then the triumph of the therapeutic is probably permanent.

Well then, can we be good without God? Certainly some people could. Marcus Aurelius, David Hume, George Eliot, John Stuart Mill, and William James—my own candidates for the five most perfect human beings—were not theists. But of course, the existence of exceptions has never been at issue. The question is about the rest of us, run-of-the-mill humanity. What can motivate ordinary men and women to behave decently most of the time and heroically in emergencies?

Perhaps it might help to reduce the many temptations to behave otherwise. Chief among these in twenty-first-century America are the relentless sexualization of advertising and entertainment, the pervasive economic insecurity engineered by business and governmental (especially Republican) policies, and the enfeeblement of civic life entailed by extreme laissez-faire ideology. These things make it harder to maintain dignity or restraint and to trust or care about other people. None of them are necessary consequences of skepticism or intellectual freedom, and some of them are promoted most vigorously by people who loudly proclaim themselves religious. Only the first of them has provoked any organized religious opposition, however, and even then has generated only a fraction of the energy and resources wasted on opposing sex education and the teaching of evolution—not to mention the anti-abortion movement, which would surely prevent more abortions by helping to lower the sexual temperature of consumer marketing than by proselytizing unwed mothers and harassing their physicians.

Just as important as avoiding temptation is acquiring the strength to subdue it. Ordinary people must become heroes, and we can. The deepest determinant of contemporary social psychology is not mass unbelief but mass production. Industrialism has decisively undermined the republican ideals of independence, self-sufficiency, and proprietorship—the "modest competence" postulated by early democratic theorists as the basis of civic virtue and civil equality. It is the practice of demanding skills, rather than fragmented and routinized drudgery, that disciplines us and makes mutual respect and sympathy possible. Work that provides scope for the exercise of virtues and talents; a physical, social, and political environment commensurate in scale with our authentic, non-manufactured needs and appetites; and a much greater degree of equality, with fewer status distinctions, and those resting on inner qualities rather than money—these are the requirements of psychic health at present. The alternative is infantilism and authoritarianism, compensated—at least until the earth's ecology breaks down—by frantic consumption.

Tracing a society's predicament to its historical and political roots is more difficult than endlessly excoriating or mocking its most outlandish manifestations. It is also more rewarding. That is why, after reading *Freud: The Mind of the Moralist* and perhaps also *The Triumph of the Therapeutic*, those in sympathy with Rieff's complaint should turn away from his own writings to those of Christopher Lasch. In a series of invaluable books, notably *The Minimal Self* (1984), *The True and Only Heaven* (1991), and *The Revolt of the Elites* (1995), Lasch diagnosed contemporary narcissism far more rigorously and persuasively than Rieff. It is the worker's loss of autonomy, Lasch showed, his dependence on a remote, centralized economic authority, that has produced a culture of unlimited consumption and ersatz self-expression; and it is the disappearance of the household economy, which removed the father's work life from the child's experience, that has produced the characteristic modern ambivalence about authority, which Rieff can only blame on rationalist hubris and original sin. Lasch's exceptional historical insight, along with his robust, unflagging concern with democracy and equality, set him, morally as well as intellectually, above all other recent critics of modernity.

Lasch has also, it happens, written the best essay I have encountered about Rieff, a chapter in *The Revolt of the Elites*. After much agreement and praise, he gently rebuked Rieff for falling into a practice the older man had himself rightly criticized: i.e., recommending religion for purely instrumental reasons. "The issue," Lasch reminded Rieff, "is not whether religion is necessary but whether it is true." For that reason, "an honest atheist is always to be preferred to a culture Christian." Notwithstanding Rieff's uncompromising anathemas, honest believers and honest unbelievers will need one another if contemporary American society is to be redeemed.

Inwardness

If all thinkers are either foxes or hedgehogs, then Kierkegaard was decidedly a hedgehog. By his own emphatic acknowledgment, everything he wrote had a single purpose: to arouse a certain state of mind, or soul, in each of his readers. He called this state of mind "the consciousness of sin." What he meant by that is something like what St. Augustine and Martin Luther meant, but not exactly. In the differences lie his originality and his importance for us.

The Present Age was written in 1846. You might reasonably expect that a book so titled would offer some clue to the age in which it was written, yet there is nary a word or phrase in *The Present Age* by means of which we might infer with any confidence which century or continent it was composed in. It could have appeared anywhere in the Western Hemisphere at any time in the last two hundred years.

But only in the West, and only in the last two centuries. *The Present Age* is a stellar entry in the genre of anti-modern manifesto, an early landmark in the still far-from-exhausted intellectual backlash against democracy, science, and unbelief. Kierkegaard did not get around to railing at democracy or science very much—he died too young—but his hostility to secular rationalism was implacable, and far more subtle than that of most other defenders of religious faith.

So subtle, admittedly, that it can be difficult at times to understand exactly what K. is exercised about. "Our age is essentially one of understanding and reflection, without passion, momentarily bursting into enthusiasm, and shrewdly relapsing into repose," he begins promisingly. One awaits, at first eagerly and then with mounting impatience, some concrete development of this thesis, some penetrating analysis of a typical episode in the life of mid-19th-century Europe. But there is no episode, no example, no historical reference whatever. Instead we are given a witty and caustic but relentlessly abstract psychosocial phenomenology of Enlightened Man.

For Enlightenment is the culprit. Not the actual doctrines of the 17th-century scientists and 18th-century philosophers, or that period's historical and philological criticisms of Christianity. About these Kierkegaard had virtually nothing to say, here or elsewhere. It was the process of popular enlightenment and the institutions—above all, the Press—to which it gave rise, the new culture of discussion and publicity, and the effect of all this on the psychology of the individual Christian that obsessed him.

"Ours is the age of advertisement and publicity," he complains, as a result of which "there is no more action or decision." Awareness of too many viewpoints produces paralysis, and so does the habit of seeing oneself as part of "the public," an entity hitherto unknown. Cosmopolitanism is a distraction, since there is no point in forming opinions about matters one cannot hope to influence. Opinions (as opposed to convictions, which require decision and lead to action) are in any case frivolous things. The upshot of continual discussion—the "deliberation" prized by theorists of liberal democracy—is perpetual stalemate and universal shallowness. As he put it in *Concluding Unscientific Postscript*: "If we wish to express in a single sentence the difference between ancient times and our own, we should doubtless have to say: 'In ancient times only an individual here and there knew the truth; now all know it, but the inwardness of its appropriation stands in an inverse relationship to the extent of its dissemination.'" Ultimately the individual himself disappears, swallowed up in the public. "The abstract leveling process, that self-combustion of the human race, produced by the friction which arises when the individual ceases to exist as singled out by religion, is bound to continue, like a trade wind, and consume everything."

What is this "inwardness" whose fateful disappearance Kierkegaard is prophesying? It is, for him, the only true form of life. Neither the existence of God nor any other important truth can be known with absolute certainty—to this extent Kierkegaard has abandoned orthodox Christianity and traditional metaphysics. Yet we must act in matters of ultimate significance—love, belief, vocation, morality—or else drift. The latter, according to K, is what the present age has contrived to do:

> When people's attention is no longer turned inwards, when they are no longer satisfied with their own inner religious lives, but turn to others and to things outside themselves, where the relation is intellectual, in search of that satisfaction, when nothing important ever happens to gather the threads of life together with the finality of a catastrophe: then instead we get talkativeness.

Obviously "talkativeness" includes celebrity journalism, self-help books, TV, Web-surfing, Facebook, and Twitter. Perhaps also, less obviously, psychotherapy, novel-reading, and most higher education.

Talkativeness keeps us connected and on the surface, while "silence is the essence of inwardness, of the inner life." If we go inside ourselves and remain there, we will eventually be confronted, out of our own depths, with choices, decisions, ultimate questions, which can only be resolved by an act, a leap of faith. "An objective uncertainty held fast [with] the most passionate inwardness is the truth, the highest truth attainable for an existing individual." To grasp the necessity of this existential decision, or leap of faith, is to live in what Kierkegaard called "fear and trembling" and is what he meant by the "consciousness of sin." The present age distracts us from this terrifying but soul-creating awareness. Getting and spending, texting and tweeting, we lay waste our spirits. Amid this carnival of stimuli, the soul, that dense kernel of spiritual gravity, evaporates, leaving behind a light ontological froth. "I have discovered," Pascal wrote of his age, "that all our unhappiness comes from one thing: that we cannot bear to sit in our room, alone and silent." The lightness of modern being is seductive but finally unbearable.

An Honest Believer

I never knew a Protestant or, with one exception, a Jew until I went to college. East Boston, the ethnic, inner-city, working-class community where I grew up, was as Catholic in the 1950s and early '60s as southern Italy, where most East Bostonians or their parents or (in my case) grandparents had come from. I only learned about the existence of non-Catholics from a discussion in the *Baltimore Catechism* of the conditions under which they could be saved.

While in college I joined Opus Dei, the contemporary equivalent of the sixteenth-century Society of Jesus, with all the latter's pristine Counter-Reformation rigor. Like most other members of the order, I acquired a papal certificate in Thomistic philosophy and began theological studies. But rashly, I also elected to major in modern European intellectual history, which meant continuous exposure to heresy. Today, many Catholic students—and clergy—seem able to bend to the modern gale without straining the tendons of conscience. But I could not. Living as I was the *consilia evanglii*, vetting each course reading assignment against the Index of Forbidden Books, always mindful of the conclusion of Pius IX's *Syllabus of Errors*, which condemned the proposition that "the Roman Pontiff can and should harmonize himself with progress, with liberalism, and with modern civilization," the choice for me was orthodoxy or apostasy, *sacrificium intellectus* or *sacrificium fidei*.

I sacrificed faith. For all the usual reasons, and one that may be idiosyncratic. I decided, looking back, that I had never encountered, in life or in print, a Catholic at once intelligent, honest, and fully modern. I should explain: I had ruled out Maritain and Gilson; they were primarily technical philosophers, and anyway lived in the mental atmosphere of earlier centuries. "Existential" Catholics, mainly French novelists and poets plus Graham Greene, didn't count either; they were uninterested in arguments and ceded them all to unbelievers. Evelyn Waugh was a comic genius, but intellectually trivial and politically mean.

Cardinal Newman and G. K. Chesterton came closest. But I couldn't entirely trust Newman after reading his controversy with Kingsley. Vastly cleverer, Newman won the debate on points; but Kingsley's original claim—that "truth, for its own sake, has never been a virtue with the Romish clergy"— if unproven, was yet not quite refuted, at least by Newman. Polemically, no one could lay a glove on Chesterton, but only because he never stood still. In my exasperation, I exulted over T. S. Eliot's unjust judgment: "He has a mind that swarms with ideas. I see no evidence that it thinks."

"By their fruits you will know them," Jesus said; but I didn't know of a single Catholic thinker who had wrestled with the angel of modernity and retained his or her orthodoxy for reasons I could respect. I felt I had a scriptural warrant for irreligion. I still do, on the whole—though now my doubt is troubled, there is a thorn in the side of my unbelief. I've discovered, to my discomfort, a modern Christian I admire: C. S. Lewis.*

Lewis is probably best known for his children's series, *The Narnia Chronicles*, which I haven't read, and next best known for his literary scholarship, which I haven't read either. But I may be the only atheist who has read every word of his voluminous Christian apologetics. "The key to my books," he wrote, "is Donne's maxim, 'The heresies that men leave are hated most.' The things I assert most vigorously are those that I resisted long and embraced late." The heresies Lewis left were those I embraced; and since the orthodoxies that men leave are also hated most, my relation to him could only be, or begin as, fascinated antipathy.

What particularly got under my skin was his conception of evil. Lewis was a connoisseur of evil. Not in Sadean detail, but

*Although Lewis was Anglican rather than Catholic, his writings are undoubtedly far more orthodox, from the point of the Roman Curia, than those of nominal Catholics like Hans Kung or Teilhard de Chardin.

in depth: his idea, reiterated and refined from book to book, was that insistence on autonomy is our original sin. To call one's soul one's own was his definition of damnation; in our will is our unpeace. Lewis argued relentlessly, and more plausibly than I could bear, that nihilism—the natural terminus of the modern rejection of metaphysics—is not an innocent or even a stable position, that it must lead to anomie and the war of all against all—to Hell. Recall Kant: "What is Enlightenment? It is humankind's emergence from its own, self-imposed minority." When I encountered Kant's affirmation, I thought it the most inspiring thing I had ever read; I was proud to be modern. Lewis put that pride in question. We all learn eventually about the dark side of enlightenment, but it is hard to forgive the one who first points it out to us.

Lewis's phenomenology of evil attained its apotheosis in Wither, archfiend of *That Hideous Strength*, the conclusion of his theological science-fiction trilogy. Wither was a philosopher-bureaucrat, whose mode of operation—almost a mode of being—was to blur distinctions. Now, a short definition of modern intellectual history might be: the progressive undermining of all firm distinctions, metaphysical, epistemological, and ethical. In recent years, no one has carried on this dissolution more subtly or rigorously than Richard Rorty, perhaps the most respected living Anglo-American philosopher. I revere Rorty, but thanks to Lewis, I have never been able to leave off mentally comparing him to Wither. And when I heard Rorty lecture for the first time, the physical resemblance I saw—or fancied—between him and Wither made the hair stand up on the back of my neck. That is how it feels, I suppose, when mentor and tormentor meet inside one's head.

What I dislike most about Christianity is the doctrine of Hell; and what I like most about Lewis is that, for all his orthodoxy, he disliked it too. Enough to compose what is surely the most humane portrait of Hell ever penned by a believer: *The Great Divorce*. Lewis did not deny, but could not quite accept, that finite turpitude merits infinite pain. So he imagined a continual commerce between saints and shades, the blessed and the damned, in which the former, like celestial psychotherapists, tempt the latter into surrendering their unreal, imprisoning will. The comparison (mine) with psychotherapy is not frivolous: in effect, if not in intention, Lewis suggests that Hell is neurosis. Which is true and tragic, though not quite orthodox.

To each shade in Lewis's fable comes a mentor-saint, linked to his or her earthly life in some way, to guide him or her toward Reality. *"Der Herr Gott ist raffiniert,"* Einstein conjectured, meaning "God is tricky." I hope so. Tricky enough, at any rate, to put Lewis on my case after I'm damned. I can't think who else might persuade me to give up modernity for eternity.

Only Death

"Man was created a rebel," Dostoevsky's Grand Inquisitor admonished the silent Christ in his prison cell, "and how can rebels be happy?" The burden of freedom, the responsibility of finding—or creating—one's own purpose and meaning without the guidance of authoritative inherited creeds and values, is too heavy for all but a few. The rest of us cannot endure for long the tensions of uncertainty. We must, at some point, stop questioning, quiet our doubts, turn away from moral and metaphysical inquiry and toward life. Untrammeled skepticism ends in paralysis.

That is true of societies as well as individuals. No purely rational justification can be offered for trust and self-sacrifice. But without them, social life is chaos, a war of all against all.

Until a few hundred years ago, this problem scarcely existed. The authority of communities and traditions, though often enough evaded or defied, was rarely put in radical question. There were sinners, doubters, even heretics; but dogma and hierarchy, as the foundation of individual morality and social organization, were unchallenged.

Then modernity happened. Beginning in fifteenth-century Europe, a critical, experimental, libertarian spirit began to flourish, which came to be known as "humanism." A crescendo of scientific discoveries, artistic innovations, geographical explorations, and political reforms ensued until, at the end of the eighteenth century, Kant hailed "humankind's emergence from its self-imposed minority" and baptized it "Enlightenment." At the same time, the prestige of the sacred and the supernatural, of what the Grand Inquisitor called "miracle, mystery, and authority" and declared indispensable to ordinary people's happiness, was correspondingly diminished.

In the nineteenth and twentieth centuries, humanism's luster was tarnished. First came the blight of early industrialization, then colonial brutality, totalitarian repression, and the technologies of extermination in concentration camps and global wars. Even after these horrors passed, in the midst of unprecedented prosperity, an epidemic of spiritual emptiness descended: alienation, consumerism, and the loneliness of mass society. Perhaps, as a minority of modern thinkers have always believed, we cannot live by reason alone. Perhaps modernity is a mistake.

Criticism of modernity is a distinguished intellectual tradition. In the first half of the twentieth century, Max Weber, Hannah Arendt, Theodor Adorno, and Max Horkheimer formulated such criticisms with great subtlety and learning, as have Christopher Lasch, Philip Rieff, Alasdair MacIntyre, and John Gray more recently. The Australian sociologist John Carroll makes a small but significant addition to this tradition with *The Wreck of Western Culture*,* published in 1993 but now revised and appearing for the first time in the United States.

Carroll is not your usual sociologist. Not only does he not make a fetish of data and method; he eschews them altogether. *The Wreck of Western Culture* is nothing so pedestrian as social theory; it is a (sometimes) inspired vaticination, a dramatic and portentous reading of the entrails of Western high culture from Homer to Hollywood. Proceeding from one representative masterwork to the next, Carroll meditates them intensely, laying siege to each one's inner meaning, pitting them against one another, and wresting from the sequence a hidden narrative of Western decline. It is an audacious performance, sometimes electrifying but just as often erratic and tendentious. It is hard not to be frequently impressed, but even harder not to be continually exasperated.

Boldly (or rashly), Carroll begins with a proclamation of universal ruin. "Our culture is a flat expanse of rubble." In our depths, we "are desperate, yet don't care much anymore. We are timid, yet we cannot be shocked. We are inert underneath

*Intercollegiate Studies Institute, 2009.

our busyness. We are destitute in our plenty. We are homeless in our own homes." If you do not recognize yourself in this desolate portrait, you will simply have to take Carroll's word for its accuracy; no attempt is made to substantiate, or even elaborate on, the book's initial, apocalyptic paragraph.

Not diagnosis but etiology is Carroll's concern. How have we arrived at this civilizational cul de sac? It started five centuries ago, Carroll answers, with our adoption of the false myth of humanism. The ambition of humanism was "to found an order on earth in which freedom and happiness prevailed, without any transcendental or supernatural supports—an entirely human order." In humanism's glory days, the eras of Socrates, Leonardo, and Newton, this was a pardonable illusion. But now, in the wake of Auschwitz, the Gulag, Hiroshima, and 9/11, the bankruptcy of humanism is manifest. We need a new cultural myth. Since none is yet available, Carroll proposes to sift through the wreckage, retracing the path to catastrophe and prospecting for glimmers of a different future.

Before Socrates, the Greeks were not humanists, they were fatalists. The gods—and behind them, a dimly discerned cosmic order—determined human destiny. Philosophical speculation about the good life and right action was irrelevant; culture rested on *mythos*, the "timeless archetypal narratives that carry the eternal truths," the "ancient currents of shape and form that move in the unconscious dreamtime of the people." Myths and stories give a culture and its members "a place to stand"—an indispensable function, which mere human reason and will cannot fulfill.

Likewise, reason and will cannot withstand the annihilating necessity of death. But Jesus's resurrection was "the death of death": that is, an end to death as the meaning, or negation, of life. For Carroll, Jesus's key affirmations are "Before Abraham came to be, I am" and "I am the way, the truth, and the life." With these, he offered himself as a place to stand, transcending the Law. His disciples Paul, Luther, and Calvin would become humanism's greatest opponents.

The first humanist masterpiece Carroll ponders is Donatel-lo's fifteenth-century sculpture of a Venetian general on horse-back, the *Gattamelata*. The figure's ease, grace, and power "anticipate the Renaissance ideal, 'we can become what we will,' and project it in three-dimensional form." The *virtu* embodied in the *Gattamelata* also animates Brutus in Shake-speare's *Julius Caesar*. Brutus acts; Hamlet, famously, does not. The two plays are the day and night sides of "humanism's quintessential genius."

In *Hamlet* and Hans Holbein's painting, *The Ambassadors*, a skull appears. This is the sort of detail from which Carroll conjures far-reaching interpretations of cultural health or mal-aise. The gravedigger scene in *Hamlet* is not merely a comic interlude; the *trompe l'oeil* skull in *Ambassadors* is not merely a visual trick. On the contrary, Carroll claims, their significance is momentous. "When culture is reduced to the skull, death takes over. . . . Once faith is gone, fate is reduced to necessity—and the ultimate necessity is death." In Carroll's reading, the painting and the play acknowledge that "there is no humanist solution."

The Protestant Reformation is usually seen as a religious parallel to the Renaissance, a movement of liberation from authority and tradition. Carroll sees it differently. Luther opposed faith and grace to reason and will; he and Calvin "preached darkness and suffering against the reasonable and the comfortable." Against the hope, common to secular and Catholic humanism, that a measure of wisdom and righteous-ness might be attained through human effort, Luther and Cal-vin insisted on our radical depravity, folly, and helplessness.

Through lengthy commentaries on paintings by Rem-brandt, Vermeer, Poussin, and Velazquez, Carroll traces the achievements and failures of the Protestant Reformation and its less well-known Catholic counterpart. Descartes and Kant advanced the humanist project, undermining notions of cosmic order and setting reason in command of philosophy. Bach and Jane Austen founded their art on perceptions of human insuf-ficiency and dependence. Kierkegaard and Nietzsche subjected themselves fully, heroically, to the spiritual tensions between humanist light and anti-humanist darkness. After them, the deluge: the frank "degradation of Western culture," illustrated by Edvard Munch's *Madonna* and Marcel Duchamp's *Urinal*. In its "death throes," the only vital works that Western culture yields are futile protests against modern homelessness, either ironic (the novels of Henry James) or wistful (the movies of John Ford).

Undoubtedly, to produce—in fewer than 300 pages—a passionate, imaginative, richly detailed interpretation of the spiritual history of the modern West is not a small achievement, even if that interpretation is, as I believe, profoundly wrong. At a time when cutting-edge cultural criticism is often about ephemeral effluvia, it apparently takes a maverick Aussie sociologist to don the prophet's mantle. Let us praise him, then, if only for forcing us to look once again at our cultural monuments, this time as harbingers of life or death.

But is it true that "without God, without a transcendental law, there is only death"? And—an entirely separate question— even if that *is* true, does that make it any more likely that either God or a transcendental law actually does exist? Like virtually all other anti-modernists, Carroll does not even assert—much less attempt to prove—the existence of God or transcendental law. He merely deplores the consequences of not believing in them. This is not, it seems to me, a grown-up position.

In any case, perhaps there are grounds for a truce between believers and unbelievers. Why not lay aside questions of ultimate meaning for as long as there is unnecessary suffering in the world? I don't mean necessary suffering, like disappointed love or the infirmities of age. I mean wholly unnecessary suffering, like that of the billion or two (no one really knows) people who are undernourished, illiterate, or without shelter, sanitation, clean water, or medical and dental care. When there are no more such, then let us begin asking again about the meaning of life and the existence of God.

The Realm of Freedom

Lewis Hyde, a gifted poet and translator, has had trouble making a living. This experience has led him to reflect on our current social arrangements, in which to do one's best work—to
offer one's most precious gifts—may bring no return. The irrationality of these arrangements—competition and commodity
production—has occurred to nearly everyone, if only in passing,
and has goaded a great many people into print. Yet Hyde has
original and fruitful things to say in this wise, charming, wide-
ranging book.*

The Gift is in part a history of the world we have lost, the
world before the hegemony of the market. From ethnography
and folklore, Hyde has reconstructed the economics and ethos
of societies based on gift exchange. Trade is immemorial, of
course; but production for a market, as an organizing principle
of society, is new, as is the ethos of such a society: possessive
individualism. Far more typical of human history is the circulation of goods and services on something like the following principles. First, social status is conferred not by wealth
accumulated but by wealth disbursed. The "big man" is the
one who throws the biggest parties, or whose ceremonial gifts
are of exceptional quality and quantity. Second, "the gifts must
always move": the reception of gifts or favors creates recipro-
cal obligations, though not exclusively to the donor. Everyone
is embedded in a network of such obligations, so that in fact,
as well as in theory, everything everyone possesses is owed to
everyone else. Third, the material basis of the group's life—
game, fish, fruit, trees, children—is considered a gift, for which
mythical explanations, rites of thanksgiving, and rules of use
must be formulated and administered, usually by priests. And

*The Gift: Imagination and the Erotic Life of Property. Random House, 1983.

so on, with all such principles giving expression to the primacy of the collective.

The anthropological record is sparse, so Hyde reconstructs a good deal of the ethos of pre-modernity from fairy tales. In the relevant tales, a magical gift is given to one person, it is hoarded, and disaster ensues; a similar gift is given to a second person, it is shared, and that person is superabundantly rewarded. The many variations on this theme occasionally hint at different attitudes of giftedness and gratitude, but the morality of the tales is invariable: the generous are disproportionately rewarded and the selfish are disproportionately punished.

Hyde then offers a history of humankind's fall from grace: a history of usury. Usury—lending at interest—contravenes the ethics of a gift society: wealth must not be removed from circulation; all wealth belongs to the group; no person's gift may become another person's capital. The prohibition of usury was virtually unanimous in both religious and early civil society. But by the middle of the nineteenth century, nearly all usury laws had been repealed and the theology of usury, at least in industrial societies, had altered drastically. Somehow the possessive individualism on which capitalist ideology is based had crept into Protestant theology and become ethical individualism, with its radical devaluation of the spiritual authority of the church. It is a fascinating chapter of intellectual history, masterfully narrated here.

And yet the material Hyde has culled from ethnography, folklore, and religious history is open to a very different reading. On his own evidence and that of his main sources (in particular, Marshall Sahlins' *Stone Age Economics*), gift societies were—to exaggerate only slightly—Hobbesian societies. Gift exchange was, at least in part, a way of keeping the war of all against all in abeyance. Hyde understates the element of involuntary obligation and implicit sanction in the "institutions of positive reciprocity" he praises. Gift exchange among the Kwakuitl sounds a lot like hug exchange in California: something you do not out of spontaneous affection, but because if you don't you're considered antisocial. Arguably, the purpose of gift-giving in pre-modern societies is not to bear witness to a lively sense of loving community but to create a plausible appearance of it and to shore up that facsimile against the dimly sensed disintegrative possibilities of individualism: envy, possessiveness, self-aggrandizement. Like the practices of Christian asceticism, the rituals of gift exchange are to some extent defenses, or more precisely, reaction-formations.

Fairy tales obviously embody some of the worst as well as the best wisdom of the race. It is characteristic of the moral and psychological poverty of pre-modernity that in the tales Hyde cites, the victims—those who are too insecure and unhappy to give freely, to part with the gift—are blamed and further deprived, while the emotionally rich get richer, as if their generosity were not, like all virtue in a world of scarcity, an accident of temperament and upbringing.

In a chapter on "The Gift Community" and thereafter (the latter half of *The Gift* includes long studies of Whitman and Pound), Hyde overcomes temptations to romanticize pre-modernity and begins in earnest to grapple with the tensions that give his subject point and poignancy. Like all ancient institutions, gift exchange embodies hopes of rootedness, connectedness, mutuality, spontaneity, surrender—the benefits of *eros*. Market exchange, for all its world- and soul-destroying irrationality, embodies complementary hopes: mobility, separateness, individuality, self-possession—the benefits of *logos*. And these polarities suggest others: criticism/myth, innovation/conservatism, rights/responsibilities, masculine/feminine. Hyde skillfully elicits one set of meanings after another from historical changes in modes of production and exchange, reckoning psychic loss and gain with keen discrimination.

But what is to be done? Gift exchange, or primitive anarcho-communism, is no longer a possible form of social organization; it could flourish only within small, self-sufficient groups. In industrial society one can try to draw boundaries, to mark off privileged spheres—friendship, family, art, collective political work—within which commodity logic may be suspended and something like gift relations may operate. But commodity logic is relentless; in the end, someone must enter the market economy in order to support the privileged sphere.

How much of the spirit of the gift can be preserved? Hyde suggests that we look for an answer in the psychology of creativity and in the social relations of art and science. *The Gift* contains an exquisite evocation of what Hyde calls "creative commerce" and "the labor of gratitude." Among colleagues, inspiration and example are paid for not by a fee but by the self-transformation of the recipient. The distributional premises of a competitive market economy are scarcity and the zero-sum. But to the extent that ideas circulate as gifts, the "wealth" of every individual in a cooperative creative "economy"—in an art or a science—increases simultaneously. And so, in a limited and fragile way, it really is true of the community of scientists and artists that "the free development of each is a condition of the free development of all."

This is an idealized portrait, of course; the egotism of actual artists and scientists is familiar enough. But that idealization at least suggests the right questions. What are the material conditions of creative freedom? Are freedom and justice best conceived as rights to full membership in a creative community? How would a world of artists, respectful of one another's gifts, organize their collective subsistence labor? This is what political theory, too often a sink of portentous obscurity and spurious rigor, ought to be about.

The Gift does not pretend to rigor, It is no more than a sustained meditation, full of gaps and perplexities, intriguing hints, tentative suggestions, and above all, generous hopes. Still, if only as a memory and a prophecy, a glimpse from the realm of necessity into a realm of freedom, it is, like the best of gifts, good beyond expectation, beyond desert.

The Radicalism of Tradition

Simone de Beauvoir wrote of the 20th-century conservative thinker: "Gloomy or arrogant, he is the man who says no; his real certainties are all negative. He says no to modernity, no to the future, no to the living action of the world; but he knows that the world will prevail over him." That T. S. Eliot at least partly resembled this imaginary portrait he himself acknowledged; as he wrote to a friend in 1921: "Having only contempt for every existing political party, and profound hatred for democracy, I feel the blackest gloom." In daily life, it is true, Eliot was neither gloomy nor arrogant but serene and gracious, generous and humble. At the height of his fame, his courtesy even to the callow and importunate was legendary. Yet however Eliot achieved this extraordinary equableness (if in fact he did—Randall Jarrell speculated that he was actually "one of the most subjective and demonic poets who ever lived, the victim and helpless beneficiary of his own inexorable compulsions and obsessions"), he doubtless saw himself as a man whose vocation was to say no, to stand athwart history strenuously wielding negative certainties.

No to what? Why, exactly, did Eliot loathe modernity and what, exactly, did he hope to conserve against its advance? In *After Strange Gods* (which remains, notwithstanding the infamous remark about "freethinking Jews," an important statement of Eliot's beliefs), he refers to "the living death of modern material civilization" and declares "Liberalism, Progress, and Modern Civilization" self-evidently contemptible. (The latter, perhaps, was an echo of the mighty conclusion of Pius IX's *Syllabus of Errors*, which condemned the proposition that "the Roman Pontiff can, and ought to, reconcile himself to, and come to terms with, progress, liberalism and modern civilization.") Elsewhere in the same vein Eliot deplores "the immense panorama of futility and anarchy which is contemporary history" and lays it down that "one can assert with some confidence that our period is one of decline." He praised Baudelaire who, in an age of "programmes, platforms, scientific progress, humanitarianism, and revolutions," of "cheerfulness, optimism, and hopefulness," understood that "what really matters is Sin and Redemption" and perceived that "the possibility of damnation is so immense a relief in a world of electoral reform, plebiscites, sex reform, and dress reform . . . that damnation itself is an immediate form of salvation—of salvation from the ennui of modern life, because it gives some significance to living."

At the root of this harsh condemnation of modernity lay the conviction of sin—Original Sin. Eliot believed that most people have very little intelligence or character. Without firm guidance from those who have more of both, the majority are bound to reason and behave badly. Eliot made this point frequently: sometimes gently, as in the well-known line from "Burnt Norton": "Humankind cannot bear very much reality"; sometimes harshly, as in "The Function of Criticism," where he derided those in whom democratic reformers place their hopes as a rabble who "ride ten in a compartment to a football match at Swansea, listening to the inner voice, which breathes the eternal message of vanity, fear, and lust."

The obtuseness and unruliness of humankind in the mass meant that order, the prime requisite of social health, could only be secured by subordination to authority, both religious and political. "For the great mass of humanity . . . their capacity for *thinking* about the objects of their faith is small"—hence the need for orthodoxy and an authoritative church rather than an illusory Inner Voice. Likewise, "in a healthily stratified society, public affairs would be a responsibility not equally borne"— hence the need for a hereditary governing class. Underlying these social hierarchies is a hierarchy of values. "Liberty is good, but more important is order, and the maintenance of order justifies any means."

Order, long preserved, produces tradition: "all the actions, habits, and customs," from the most significant to the most conventional, that "represent the blood kinship of 'the same people living in the same place.'" Eliot's best-known discussions of tradition are found in his literary essays: "Tradition and the Individual Talent," "The Metaphysical Poets," and others. His poetry was, of course, revolutionary as well as conservative, and his criticism explains this apparent paradox. Artistic originality emerges only after a lengthy assimilation of many traditions. The artist surrenders his individuality, and it is returned to him enriched. The tradition too is enriched. "The whole existing order" is "if ever so slightly, altered; and so the relations, proportions, values of each work of art toward the whole are readjusted; and this is conformity between the old and the new.... The past [is] altered by the present as much as the present is directed by the past."

A continually altering tradition is not an unchanging magisterium. In politics and religion as well as in poetry, Eliot's conception of tradition is surprisingly dynamic. Our "danger," he wrote, is "to associate tradition with the immovable; to think of it as something hostile to all change; to aim to return to some previous condition which we imagine as having been capable of preservation in perpetuity." On the contrary, "tradition without intelligence is not worth having." We must "use our minds" to discover "what is the best life for us . . . as a particular people in a particular place; what in the past is worth preserving and what should be rejected; and what conditions, within our power to bring about, would foster the society that we desire." This obviously does not sound like Condorcet or Godwin; but neither does it sound much like Burke or de Maistre.

Eliot was too subtle not to recognize (and too honest not to acknowledge) that his more general pronouncements about political philosophy were unsatisfactory. Like most general pronouncements, they reduce to truisms. Continuity is best, except where change is necessary. Much tradition, some innovation. Firm principles, flexibly adapted. His often-cited remark (in praise of Aristotle) that "the only method is to be very intelligent" helps in estimating his own political criticism.

Concerning two matters of large contemporary relevance, Eliot was profoundly, though unsystematically, intelligent. Eliot's political utterances were, for the most part, fragmentary and occasional: occurring in essays, lectures, and the regular "Commentaries" in his great quarterly *The Criterion*. His compliment to Henry James—"he had a mind so fine no idea could violate it"—applied to Eliot as well, for better and worse. He was never doctrinaire; but on the other hand, he was rarely definite. As one commentator observes: "To gesture toward, but not to reveal; to pursue, but not to unravel, this is Eliot's procedure." But although he eschewed programs, there is much matter in his asides.

About economics, he repeatedly professed theoretical incomprehension. But just as often, he professed skepticism that any immutable laws of political economy proved that extremes of wealth and poverty were inevitable or that state action to counter disadvantage must be futile. Disarmingly, he acknowledged:

> I am confirmed in my suspicion that conventional economic practice is all wrong, but I can never understand enough to form any opinion as to whether the particular prescription or nostrum proffered is right. I cannot but believe that there are a few simple ideas at bottom, upon which I and the rest of the unlearned are competent to decide according to our several complexions; but I cannot for the life of me ever get to the bottom.

Nevertheless, "about certain very serious facts no one can dissent." For "the present system does not work properly, and more and more are inclined to believe both that it never did and that it never will."

What were some of these indisputable "very serious facts"?

> . . . the hypertrophy of Profit into a social ideal, the distinction between the *use* of natural resources and their exploitation, the advantages unfairly accruing to the trader in contrast to the primary producer, the misdirection of the financial machine,

the iniquity of usury, and other features of a commercialized society.

Sometimes he wondered whether Western society was "assembled round anything more permanent than a congeries of banks, insurance companies and industries, and had any beliefs more essential than a belief in compound interest and the maintenance of dividends." On one occasion he sounded almost like a communist:

> Certainly there is a sense in which Britain and America are more democratic than [Nazi] Germany; but on the other hand, defenders of the totalitarian system can make out a plausible case for maintaining that what we have is not democracy but financial oligarchy.

Indeed, Eliot was full of surprises on the subject of communism. Try to imagine his drearily predictable acolytes at *The New Criterion* saying something like this:

> I have . . . much sympathy with communists of the type with which I am here concerned [i.e. "those young people who would like to grow up and believe in something"]. I would even say that . . . there are only a small number of people living who have achieved the right *not* to be communists.

Eliot did not think much of most anti-communists, who "abhor extreme socialism for motives in which a very little Christianity is blended with a great deal of self-interest and prejudice." For "no one is any more justified in a general condemnation of the principles of the extreme Left than he is in a general condemnation of those of the extreme Right. The principle of Justice affirmed by the intellectuals of the Left is at least analogous to Christian justice."

In fact, Eliot feared and despised unrestrained capitalism. He associated himself with those who "object to the dictatorship of finance and the dictatorship of bureaucracy under whatever political name it is assembled," and he delivered this tart verdict on the corporate Masters of the Univers:

Unrestrained industrialism, then (with its attendant evils of over-production, excessive "wealth," an irrelevance and lack of relation of production to consumption which it attempts vainly to overcome by the nightmare expedient of "advertisement"), destroys the upper classes first. You cannot make an aristocrat out of a company chairman, though you can make him a peer.

The indictment continues. Capitalism "is imperfectly adapted to every purpose except that of making money; and even for money-making it does not work very well, for its rewards are neither conducive to social justice nor even proportioned to intellectual ability." It "tends to divide the community into classes based upon differences of wealth and to occasion a sense of injustice among the poorer members of society." During World War II he wrote a friend that he was willing to join a "revolution" whose "enemies" would include "popular demagogues and *philosophes*" on the one hand, and on the other "those who want after this war to revert to money hegemony, commercial rivalry between nations, etc."

Even when deploring the consequences of Original Sin, Eliot could not help acknowledging the social scaffolding of moral and cultural questions. He supported censorship of pornography, though not of "books possessing, or even laying claim to, literary merit." And, he went on, "what is more insidious than any censorship is the steady influence which operates silently in any mass society organized for profit, for the depression of standards of art and culture." He was no feminist, propounding these scandalously sexist rhetorical questions: "Might one suggest that the kitchen, the children, and the church could be considered to have a claim upon the attention of married women? Or that no normal married woman would prefer to be a wage-earner if she could help it?" But at least he remembered to add: "What is miserable is a system that makes the dual wage necessary—as it is for most families in contemporary America."

The incompatibility between untrammeled capitalism and Eliot's conception of the good society went deep. "Stability is obviously necessary," he insisted—indeed it would seem to be the alpha, if not the omega, of any intelligible conservatism. "You are hardly likely to develop tradition, except where the bulk of the population is so well off where it is that it has no incentive or pressure to move about." But without precisely that incentive, the labor market of neoclassical economic theory cannot function. Stable communities or "efficient" labor markets—one must choose.

Eliot was ready to choose. An Anglican committee report he co-authored in the late 1930s called for the "thorough reconstruction of the present economic and political system." Eliot was careful with words, so he probably meant what he said here, bromidic as it sounds. A few years earlier he co-signed a letter to the *Times* arguing that there was enough wealth in the world "to give every individual a certainty of adequate provision," but that "there appears to be lacking some machinery of distribution" to accomplish this. Eliot was a redistributionist.

What kind of "economic and political system" did Eliot want? A Christian society, of course—his critique of capitalism strikingly parallels that of *Rerum Novarum, Centesimus Annus,* and other papal encyclicals. But like those venerable documents, Eliot's writings, though they could be pointedly negative, were not vividly affirmative. He thought there should be a lot more people living on the land. He thought most people should have to spend fewer hours working for a living. He enthusiastically endorsed this description of the goal: a "new type of society, which would give fullest scope both to the individual—thus securing the utmost variety in human affairs—and to the social whole—thus stimulating the rich, collective activities which would surely come to life in a society free to express its invention, its mechanical skill, its sense of the earth in agriculture and crafts, its sense of play." This sounds much more like William Morris than like Margaret Thatcher. But beyond these, he offered virtually no details. He was neither a visionary nor an activist but a critic.

《∗》

«∗»

I said above that Eliot has much to teach us about two matters of contemporary relevance. About the first—capitalism and distributive justice—he wrote much, directly if not programmatically. About the other, he wrote scarcely a word; not surprisingly, since it was hardly visible on the horizon before his death. I'm referring to the steady erosion of inwardness (Eliot would have said "spiritual depth") resulting from the omnipresence of commercial messages (the "nightmare" of "advertisement") and electronic media.

I have no doubt that Eliot would have reacted strongly and negatively to this development, so discordant with his sensibility and practice. As described in his critical essays, the gradual surrender of the artist's personality to tradition, which is at the same time the mastery and (however modest) transformation of tradition, resembles the attitude of the narrator of his *Four Quartets* toward Being and history. In both cases, the prescribed motions of the spirit are inward and downward, the virtues prescribed are humility, gravity, receptiveness. The refrain of "Burnt Norton" has become a meme: "the still point of the turning world."

This capacity—as a valiant minority of contemporary critics keep insisting—is what advertising and the cyberworld are, with fearful rapidity, extinguishing. It simply cannot withstand the immediacy, volume, and near-instantaneous succession of stimuli to which all of us outside a monastery are incessantly subjected. The spirit has its rhythm and metabolism; it cannot survive in just any environment. Or, if you prefer: the brain is plastic and may be drastically reshaped. Our world is flat, as we have been loudly and monotonously told. Will the same processes that flattened it also flatten our souls?

The most moving passage I have encountered in all of Eliot's writings occurs in a letter to his dear friend Paul Elmer More:

To me, religion has brought at least the perception of something above morals, and therefore extremely terrifying; it has brought me not happiness, but the sense of something above happiness and therefore more terrifying than ordinary pain and misery; the very dark night and the desert. To me, the phrase "to be damned for the glory of God" is sense and not paradox; I had far rather walk, as I do, in daily terror of eternity, than feel that this was only a children's game in which all the contestants would get equally worthless prizes in the end. . . . And I don't know whether this is to be labeled "Classicism" or "Romanticism"; I only think that I have hold of the tip of the tail of something quite real, more real than morals, or than sweetness and light and culture.

This revelation has not been vouchsafed to me, but I can recognize here a description of something supremely valuable. I would fight, as I believe Eliot would, to preserve the conditions of its possibility against the encroachment of the electronic Hive.

Flatheads of the World, Unite

In *Beyond Good and Evil,* Nietzsche inveighed against "socialist dolts and flatheads"—positive thinkers who would tidy up the chaos wrought by the devaluation of all values, preaching a new form of salvation and assuring everyone that conflict, perhaps even "suffering itself," is merely "something that must be abolished." It was not only their dream of reconciliation and community that offended Nietzsche; it was their piety, their sentimentality, their conventionality, their opportunism. Socialist humanism was bogus, he concluded disgustedly: "the democratic movement is the heir of the Christian movement."

Michael Harrington is nothing if not a positive thinker. For some time he has been America's most visible and energetic social democrat, spiritual leader of a doughty, beleaguered sect who now call themselves the Democratic Socialists of America. This is a fallow period for democratic socialist politics, so Harrington has turned, for the interim, to other tasks. His latest book* is personal, pastoral, and ecumenical: a testament, an attempt to shore up the faith of the believing band, and an effort to bring the socialist evangel to the "morally serious"—to all those grieved (rather than relieved) by the "spiritual crisis of Western Civilization."

The crisis in question is the death of God, at least in his Judeo-Christian manifestation. That is a large and familiar story, and Harrington concentrates on one part of it: the political consequences of the decline of institutional religion. The Christian God was not only a mighty fortress and most holy Light, but also a principle of order, fountainhead of authority, summit and guarantor of a Great Chain of Legitimacy.

*The Politics at God's Funeral: The Spiritual Crisis of Western Civilization by Michael Harrington. Holt, Rinehart & Winston, 1983.

Hegel, Marx, Weber, Durkheim, and many others have theorized about the social origins and functions of religion. From this dense thicket of intellectual history Harrington extracts and emphasizes the point that religion was always something more than a ruling-class plot; or as Durkheim put it, "a human institution cannot rest upon an error and a lie." The truth of Judeo-Christianity—its social truth—was solidarity, the dream of a universal community unified in value and belief.

But that solidarity rested too much on subjugation and superstition, and so was ripe for subversion by science and capitalism. The best thing in *The Politics at God's Funeral* is an account of why capitalism developed into "the first 'structurally agnostic' social formation." Its rulers having found a way to extract the social surplus "behind the backs" of all concerned, through "voluntary" market exchanges, the capitalist polity can dispense with archaic ideologies of cosmic hierarchy and divine right. Harrington explains, rather better than Irving Kristol or Michael Novak, why capitalism and democracy have often managed, however uneasily, to coexist.

In the West, epistemology replaced ontology, interests replaced ideals, bureaucracies replaced aristocracies and priesthoods. Methodological individualism became the ideology of politics. Without a public function, religion became more and more a private matter, no longer the organizing principle of public life but a refuge from it. This, in broad strokes, is the meaning of "secularization." It is, I repeat, an extremely familiar story. Harrington's rendition is competent but unoriginal and is mainly intended to motivate the most important part of the book: his "prolegomena to a political morality."

Individualism, he reminds us, clearly won't do. As the public world grows more complex, interdependence is inescapable; but untempered competitiveness makes interdependence difficult, if not impossible. In the absence of moral community and a widely shared ethic of responsibility, the individual costs of not bribing, not engineering obsolescence, not maximizing capital mobility (i.e., wrecking established communities) can be prohibitive. Yet when generally adopted, these practices impose general costs, including societal breakdown.

Where is that moral community, that ethic, to come from? Not from liberalism, which—even in its social-democratic form—can only offer a patchwork of incentives and sanctions. The modern welfare state, in words that Harrington quotes from Fred Hirsch's *Social Limits to Growth,* "involves the progressive extension of explicit social organization without the support of a matching social morality—more rules for the common good, having to be preached and adhered to in a culture oriented increasingly to the private good."

As modernity's many critics have shown, only solidarity can keep a complex society functioning. The solidarity envisioned by conservatives is based on traditionalist illusions, while liberalism does not even aspire to solidarity. What might socialist solidarity be based on? Unfortunately, having raised this all-important question, Harrington mumbles a few platitudes about "participation" arid "consensus," invokes a "united front of believers and atheists in search of a common transcendental," and brings the service to a close.

It is a disappointing ending to a promising book. Other, more daring contemporary social theorists have posed the same utopian question and worked out ambiguous or incomplete but suggestive answers. Ernest Callenbach has proposed that we take the biological phenomena of embeddedness and the stable state as social paradigms. Lewis Hyde has wondered whether the relations of artistic and scientific colleagues might serve as a model for societal relations. Marshall Berman has reminded us of the uses of modern disorder and speculated that a commitment to our own—and one another's—development may bring us together through the modernist whirlwind. And Paul Goodman used to insist that the ultimate revolutionary utopian demand is simply the freedom to do good work.

As a devout socialist flathead, I can sympathize with Harrington's desire to instill in nonbelievers the conviction of liberal or conservative sin and then bring them our amazing socialist grace. I can even admire the energy and erudition he devotes to that godly labor. But although most of the time I fervently believe that outside the democratic-socialist church there is no salvation, *The Politics at God's Funeral* is so prosaic that one sometimes yearns for a little poetry. And the poets, as we know, are of a different party.

Solidarity Ever?

We are all at least amateur philosophers of history. The cardinal category of most such philosophizing is emancipation: politically, from arbitrary authority; economically, from privilege and inherited status; intellectually, from received wisdom; morally, from convention and custom—in all cases, from restraints imposed by or in the name of some community. These installments of emancipation are the chapters in an integral grand narrative: The Growth of Freedom in the West.

In this multivolume epic, the history of the United States is often perceived as an especially glorious episode. Here, in the first (the only?) society born free, authority is suspect and the moral sovereignty of the individual is unchallenged. "Mind your own business!" and "It's a free country!": these two quintessential Americanisms are generally assumed to stand in a casual relation. And indeed, American individualism in its nobler manifestations—Shays' Rebellion, Whitman's *Democratic Vistas*, the Wobbly bards, *Seven Arts,* Dwight MacDonald's *politics,* be-bop, the Beats, feminism—has been one of the wonders of the world, one of the genuine achievements of civilization.

But progress is dialectical. Every historic advance exacts a price. Modernity—which means, among other things, the rise of a national labor market and of mass consumption—requires emancipation from the constraints on individual mobility and development entailed by pre-modern structures and values: family, locality, ethnic group, church, religious doctrine, and patriotic myth. But that which constrains may also support. Shared beliefs, loyalties, and membership create attachments among believers. These attachments are a promise of mutual aid and comfort, of a sort that money cannot buy and without which life is, for all but the most fortunate, painfully insecure. Even more important, these structures and values frame our lives, give them coherence, relieve us of the sometimes vertiginous sense of fragility and contingency to which the unaffiliated and unbelieving are vulnerable.

When insecurity and anomie are widespread, social stability is at risk. The United States has largely evaded this risk, in part because religious and civic allegiances have persisted alongside, and accommodated to, modernization. In the 1980s that accommodation came under strain, with consequences brilliantly depicted in *Habits of the Heart: Individualism and Commitment in American Life* (1985) by Robert Bellah, Richard Madsden, William Sullivan, Ann Swidler, and Steven Tipton.

Bellah et al's portrait of the contemporary American character descends from a tradition of sociological fretting about the costs of modernity. Tocqueville, Durkheim, Weber, Tonnies, the Lynds, David Riesman, Christopher Lasch, and many if not most other important modern social theorists have sounded similar themes. But what was for sociology's founders only a disturbing tendency is now a mass phenomenon. For most Americans (especially middle-class Americans, the chief subject of *Habits*), the binding force of extended and even nuclear families, neighborhoods, and regions, religious organizations, ethnic societies, and other small-to-medium-scale bodies has greatly diminished. These ties could not survive the enormous increase in residential and occupational mobility required for success within an economy and society dominated by large-scale organizations, corporate, governmental, and academic. As a result, the individual now matters far less to those she lives and works among, and vice versa. At the same time, she is likely to possess far more, materially and culturally.

Since we must all feel we matter to *someone*, we have begun to matter more to ourselves. There being fewer competing claims on us, and more resources at hand, we have taken to cultivating those selves, translating our resources into experiences and, to the extent we can afford it, into lifestyles. This is pretty much the prevailing ethos among the educated middle class. Bellah et al call it "expressive individualism" and describe its genesis, forms, and psychological effects with much subtlety and nuance.

Because expressive individualism is now so much the norm, the evocation in *Habits* of older ideals of work and citizenship is a great part of the book's value. Before work became a means of making a living and (at least for some) self-expression, it was a "calling"; that is "a practical ideal of activity and character that . . . subsumes the self into a community of disciplined practice and sound judgment [and] links a person to the larger community, in which the calling of each is a contribution to the good of all."

Similarly, citizenship was not merely a matter of advancing individual or group self-interest, as in liberal political theory and practice, but of pursuing the common good "in a society organized through public dialogue," which "can be sustained only by communities of memory, whether religious or civic." It is clear why work and citizenship so conceived would produce a very different character structure from the anxious, acquisitive, manipulative, self-protective type current in our world of bureaucracies, commodities, and universal competition.

This contrast between modern individualism and an archaic, or at least submerged, communitarianism is the organizing principle of *Habits of the Heart*. But though the authors expound the contrast forcefully and lay bare its historical roots, they decline to grasp those roots. Having identified the separation of public and private life and the "ontological individualism" of Locke as the original sins of modernity, they cannot quite bring themselves to demand repentance and conversion. Instead, eloquently but a little vaguely, they hope that "the older civic and biblical traditions have the capacity to reformulate themselves while simultaneously remaining faithful to their own deepest insights" and call for measures to "reduce the inordinate rewards of ambition and our inordinate fears of ending up as losers" (by which they mean, presumably, a more progressive tax structure and more generous social welfare programs). Amen. But will these fine sentiments vanquish the modernist Moloch?

To such complaints Bellah et al reply that they were mainly trying to get a discussion going among people of good will. The most substantial fruit of that discussion so far is *Community in America: The Challenge of 'Habits of the Heart'*, edited by Charles Reynolds and Ralph Norman.*

Like *Habits of the Heart*, *Community in America* is diverse, with contributors from across the academic landscape, from religious studies to political theory to comparative literature. In one of the book's most successful essays, Roland Delattre links addictive consumption to the dependence and anxiety generated by the "corporate culture of professionals, experts, and managers," taking military weapons procurement as an example of this dynamic. In another essay, a defense of psychoanalysis, Ernest Wallwork concedes the shallowness of the "therapeutic ethos" in its popular form but reminds us that Freud's thought retains our best guide to the scope and limits of individual autonomy. Stanley Hauerwas admonishes communitarians that Christianity can only judge or instruct, not enter dialogue with, the earthly city. Frederic Jameson offers a sophisticated postmodern-Marxist alternative reading of the situation *Habits* surveys—so sophisticated, as Bellah notes in his "Afterword" to *Community in America*, that it can scarcely have much resonance beyond a thin stratum of left-wing academic intellectuals. More tellingly, Bernard Yack argues that liberal societies have their own traditions, virtues, practices, and forms of community, which *Habits* overlooks, and that the values associated with individualism—"self-reliance, individual responsibility, and respect for constitutional authority and legal agreements"—morally integrate American society today, just as the more visibly other-directed values of the religious and republican traditions did formerly.

So ambitious a book as *Habits* is bound to leave many questions unanswered. But two would appear to be so urgent that not even the promise of a sequel seems sufficient excuse for begging the one question and evading the other. The first of

*University of California Press, 1988.

these is: What if the religious and republican traditions went into eclipse for good reasons—what if they depended on beliefs that are *not true*? The references in *Habits* to the actual content of these traditions are vague to the point of vacuousness. At one point, the authors remind the reader that "we did not create ourselves"; at another, they allude to a "covenant" between God and His people. But surely a great many even of their most sympathetic readers cannot believe in any sort of creation or covenant or God? According to *Habits*, the essence of republican virtue is devotion to the "common good." But what is there is no common good—what if the history of all hitherto existing societies *is* the history of class struggles? And what if the average modern individualist understands all this, however dimly and inarticulately, and can see no other reason—no other *philosophical* reason—not to merely eat, fuck, and be mellow?

Jeffrey Stout's contribution to *Community in America* is the only one to acknowledge that the cognitive content of the traditions *Habits* invokes somehow matters—that *Habits* may be less rather than more persuasive because of its dependence on a particular "public philosophy." There is no reason, he observes, why the authors should have sought to derive their valuable critique of American individualism from dubious philosophical first principles rather than from their splendidly thick descriptions. Not philosophical foundations but reliable reports and modest proposals are what a society in trouble needs. We should gratefully accept *Habits'* ethnography and politely ignore its theology.

There's another urgent question. The separation of public and private life is a necessary consequence of mass production and the spread of market relations. What economic changes would allow that separation to be healed, would allow work once again to be a "calling"? *Habits of the Heart* is little help here, a few inspirational passages notwithstanding. Christopher Lasch's brief but illuminating essay in *Community in America* addresses the question more straightforwardly.

Lasch takes up the Aristotelian idea (recently revived by

Alasdair MacIntyre in *After Virtue*) of "practices." Practices are activities like poetry, medicine, and sport that are ends in themselves, with internal standards of excellence and characteristic virtues. Lasch points out that while "practices have to be sustained by institutions"—e.g., medicine by hospitals, scholarship by universities—the latter "in the very nature of things tend to corrupt the practices they sustain," by rewarding practitioners with external goods like money and social status and by "subjecting [them] to standards of productivity derived from the marketplace." The purpose of liberal politics is to regulate the pursuit of self-interest; the purpose of communitarian politics, Lasch concludes, is to protect the integrity of practices.

But can the production of necessities be organized into practices? If so, how? If not, then either a good deal of the industrial system will have to go, or else some people will work at mass production and others at practices. In the former case, how much? And in the latter, how can such an arrangement be made equitable? In either case, decisions about investment and credit allocation must be made. By whom and by what criteria? In short, what social relations of production do Lasch and the authors of *Habits* have in mind? And why does one come away from both books with a suspicion that these questions would provoke a certain impatience—as though they missed the point? There are two scant references to "class" in the index of *Habits of the Heart*. "Power" does not appear at all.

The best and most useful response to *Habits* that I've encountered is a symposium comment in the *Nation* (12/28/85) by Barbara Ehrenreich. Though appreciative of the book's humane intentions and "fine dissection of the therapeutic mentality," she takes issue with its diagnosis:

> [T]he problem is not just the emptiness of middle-class life, even for the emptiest among us. The problem includes all the pain and dread that have been pressed back into the margins and final, wistful pages of *Habits of the Heart*: the hunger of the world's majority; the draining misery of most people's daily labor; torture and repression; the threat of nuclear annihilation.

> If we who are currently comfortable and affluent need a moral reference point, we will not find it in the mirror tricks of therapy *or* religion, but in other people's pain.

And also with its prescription:

> ["Socialism"] is still the only word we have that attempts to bridge the gap between our private notions of decency and morality and the public sphere of the political economy. And it is still the only vision—the only modernist vision, that is—of a world in which individual desire might be reconciled with collective need. To neglect the socialist tradition as much as Bellah and his colleagues do is to contribute to the impoverishment of the political imagination which they have so ably documented.

Ehrenreich is the author of *The Hearts of Men: American Dreams and the Flight from Commitment* (1983), which traced an evolution within American society away from "a moral climate that honored . . . responsibility, self-discipline, and a protective commitment to women and children" toward "a moral climate that endorsed irresponsibility, self-indulgence, and an isolationist detachment from the claims of others." In *The Hearts of Men* and now *Fear of Falling*,* Ehrenreich, like the authors of *Habits*, has charted "the inner life of the middle class." There is important common ground here, though also marked differences in method (social history rather than interpretive sociology), provenance (Marx rather than Tocqueville), and style (witty and direct rather than earnest and edifying).

For Bellah and his colleagues, middle-class American life represents the triumph of liberalism's emancipatory critique. Their story emphasizes the individual's liberation, for better and worse, from traditional obligations and allegiances. For Ehrenreich, modern life represents the defeat of liberalism's universalist, egalitarian aspirations. Her story is about the middle-class's growing awareness—and uneasy acceptance—of itself as an elite.

*Pantheon, 1989.

Near the end of the 19th century, the older middle class, or gentry, of independent farmers, small businessmen, self-employed lawyers, doctors, and ministers "found itself squeezed between an insurgent lower class and a powerful new capitalism." Its response was to transform itself into a "professional middle class." Professionalism created a new form of capital: "expertise," which was acquired by training and certification rather than by economic activity in the marketplace. The professions were self-regulating, which allowed them to restrict their numbers and so avoid significant competition. Also, professionals marketed themselves to business as a part of a "rational" response to labor conflict. The social sciences, social work, public health, engineering, and the new professional schools of management all gained funding and respectability by cooperating to inculcate proper attitudes in, and construct the proper environment around, an unruly working class.

This history is familiar enough. What's original in *Fear of Falling* is Ehrenreich's narrative of middle-class consciousness since the 1960s. At the beginning of that decade, the middle class chiefly inhabited suburbia, from which vantage point affluence looked so universal and secure as to seem potentially enervating. Of any "other America" they had no inkling until Michael Harrington's book of that name came to President Kennedy's attention. The resulting War on Poverty aimed not at redistributing wealth but at combating the "culture of poverty," a collection of pathologies that had supposedly kept the poor from achieving "normal" middle-class careers and living standards.

In those innocent days the poor were perceived as a manageably small category of the deprived and the deviant. Even more important, they were passive and unthreatening. Blacks mobilized by the civil rights movement were not; still, they too seemed to be demanding inclusion rather than fundamental social change. Middle-class liberals might feel considerable guilt in response to their belated discovery of poverty and discrimination. But they had no reason to feel that their societal prerogatives, their very self-definition, was being challenged.

It was the student movement, especially in its countercultural aspect, that set off their alarms. Central to the ethos of professionalism are the ideals of objectivity and rigor and the virtues of perseverance and self-denial. It was just these qualities that the poor were said to lack, evoking middle-class condescension, and that the counterculture rejected, arousing middle-class horror. For the rebellious students were largely the professional middle-class's own children, and their revolt seemed to signify the older generation's failure to reproduce itself in anything like its own image. The blame for this failure was laid to "permissiveness," an insidious and ubiquitous disease of modern civilization transmitted by a "New Class" of secular liberal intellectuals, who administered and continually enlarged the welfare state.

Ehrenreich links this preoccupation with permissiveness among neoconservatives and the New Right to the middle class's chronic "fear of falling," a "fear of inner weakness, of growing soft, of failing to strive, of losing discipline and will"—and, in consequence, losing status. There is, of course, a powerful tendency toward just this sort of narcissistic character structure in contemporary society. But its source is nothing so nebulous as "modern civilization" or so nefarious as a self-aggrandizing "New Class." Its source is the culture of consumption, promoted by advertising and essential to the health of developed capitalism. The hedonism, such as it was, of the counterculture only mirrored what Daniel Bell once described as "the hedonism stimulated by mass consumption, [without which] the very structure of business enterprises would collapse."

The New Right was of course unwilling to blame capitalism for permissiveness (or anything else). So it evolved a largely mythical ideology that counterposed the New Class, or "liberal elite," along with its underclass, minority, and "deviant" constituencies, to the virtuous and productive upholders of traditional values: business and the white working class. In the 1980s, this right-wing populism swept all before it, a half-truth whose time had come. Unsparingly but tactfully, Ehrenreich sets out the confusions besetting this worldview as it has sought desperately to reconcile the cultural contradictions of capitalism. And with equal astuteness she locates the origins of neoconservatism in the dilemma of the professional middle class, caught between its ideals of intellectual independence and public service and its need to market itself in an era of declining public expenditure and increasing corporate hegemony.

Obviously, populism can be manipulated and professionalism can rationalize privilege. But both also contain nobler possibilities: populism's instinct for justice and equality; professionalism's encouragement of curiosity and altruism. As Ehrenreich points out, there is a way to combine these qualities programmatically: interesting work for everyone. It's a demand that implies a number of others—above all, a more equal distribution of wealth, but also subsidized child care, job training and relocation, worker self-management. It connects up, too, with the idea of "practices." The Biblical/republican concept of a "calling" and the expressive-individualist ideal of "fulfilling work" may not be identical, but they have enough in common— enough political-economic prerequisites, at any rate—to sustain a stable alliance of communitarians and democratic socialists.

Unfortunately, however, most people are neither communitarians nor democratic socialists. By and large, America's elites do not believe they are morally obliged to sacrifice substantially for the sake of ordinary people. By and large, ordinary people do not believe in their own right and ability to force elites to do so. Perhaps, then—since virtually no one seems to agree with us—communitarians and socialists need to refurbish our usual answers to some fundamental questions of political morality. Why care about others? Why pay extra taxes, spend extra time, put one's status, security, children's prospects, or whatever else one cherishes, even slightly at risk? Why not remain radical individualists, each trusting to her own strength and ingenuity and to the rough justice of the marketplace?

"Because we are one Body," reply the authors of *Habits of the Heart*, "and our happiness lies in realizing our common good." "Because we are two classes," replies Ehrenreich, "and we must all suffer separately until we abolish exploitation together." These are different visions, or at least different rhetorics, of human fulfillment: on the one hand, full membership in a beloved community; on the other, equal rights in a rational collectivity. The latter is libertarian, egalitarian, secular; the former is . . . well, all those things, too, but ambivalently.

Both visions are plausible; both are honorable. Both may be irrelevant. As a species, we may simply not be up to either. The indefinite persistence of possessive individualism and bureaucratic authoritarianism seems equally likely. Perhaps the last several decades of brutally callous, mindlessly improvident, and yet generally popular leadership in the world's foremost democracy compel the attenuation, if not the abandonment, of radical hopes. "Socialism or barbarism" is the battle cry of Ehrenreich's tradition; "you cannot serve both God and mammon" is that of Bellah's. The victory—not final, perhaps, but decisive for our lifetime—of mammon and barbarism is a prospect that must haunt anyone who has lived through the Reagan/Gingrich/Bush II era.

Nothing in history or human nature guarantees that we will avoid social stasis, environmental collapse, or nuclear catastrophe. Our danger is not positive error so much as sheer unreflectiveness; not active malevolence so much as paralyzing insecurity. *Habits of the Heart* is a slight enough blow against modern anomie, as is *Fear of Falling* against class divisions. But their convergence, however partial and implicit, is encouraging. Because probably, if there is to be any ground for hope, the first requirement is the solidarity of the hopeful: communitarian and individualist, republican and socialist, religious and secular.

Growing Pains

Over the portal of modernity is written Kant's famous definition: "What is Enlightenment? It is humankind's emergence from its self-imposed childhood." But that inspiring metaphor has a sobering implication. What follows childhood, after all, is adolescence; and folklore and social science agree that, whatever its attractions, this is also the most turbulent, violent, and unhappy stage of life. If Kant's metaphor holds, humankind ought to be suffering some colossal growing pains around now.

Well, we are. In the developed countries, it's true, more people are rich than ever before—science, democracy, and capitalism have kept their promise. But more people are unhappy, too, at least by some measures, and unhappy in new ways. To simplify grandly: the traditional—indeed, immemorial—sources of unhappiness were scarcity and constraint; now, for the first time on a large scale, overstimulation and the erosion of constraint (i.e., of social bonds, which are inseparable from constraints) are also sources of unhappiness. This is not a new idea: Durkheim and Weber first conceived it and more or less founded sociology on it. But as the social consequences of modernity broaden and ramify, fresh descriptions and analyses are required of social scientists. Several such works have recently appeared, most notably Francis Fukuyama's *The Great Disruption* and Robert Putnam's *Bowling Alone,* as well as two less bold and brilliant but nonetheless valuable studies of contemporary American malaise, David Myers' *The American Paradox** and Robert Lane's *The Loss of Happiness in Market Democracies.*†

*The American Paradox: Spiritual Hunger in an Age of Plenty by David Myers, Yale Univ. Press, 2000.

†The Loss of Happiness in Market Democracies by Robert Lane. Yale Univ. Press, 2000.

Their common theme is that the way we live now has its costs. The legitimation of divorce, cohabitation, and single parenthood; the universal availability of contraception; the economic independence of women; the professionalization of child care, elder care, and other personal services; the proliferation of consumer choice; the diversification of media; the superabundance of information; the increase of residential and occupational mobility; the displacement of loyalty and personal influence by merit and competition in the workplace; the decline of party identification and patronage; the delegitimation of tradition and hierarchy, familism and governmental paternalism; and in general, the increasing prevalence of individual autonomy and economic rationality in more and more spheres of life: these are all goods. But not unmixed goods. The awkward truth appears to be that constraints are also supports, choices are also stresses, and breadth of experience may sometimes be the enemy of depth.

The data on our current "social recession" (Myers' term) are familiar, but it is useful to have them fully and clearly set out in the two books under review. Since 1960, the divorce rate has doubled. Cohabitation is seven times more frequent. Four out of 10 ninth-graders and 7 out of 10 high-school seniors report having had sexual intercourse. The average age of first marriage for men has increased from 23 to 27 and for women from 20 to 25. Births to unmarried teens have quadrupled; births to all unmarried parents have sextupled. The proportion of children not living with two parents has tripled. The number of children living with a never-married mother has increased by a factor of 13. Forty percent of all children do not live with their biological fathers.

Hours per week parents spend with children has decreased by nearly half (30 to 17). The teenage suicide rate has tripled. The rate of violent crime has quadrupled; the rate of juvenile violent crime has septupled. Twelve million people, including 3 million teenagers, contract sexually transmitted diseases each year. Average television-watching hours per household have increased 40 percent; average SAT scores have declined

50 points. The proportion of survey respondents agreeing that "most people can be trusted" has dropped 40%, while the number of those asserting that "you can't be too careful in dealing with people" has risen 50%. And although personal income has more than doubled, the proportion of Americans calling themselves "pretty well off financially" has dropped 40% and "very happy" has dropped 15%, while the incidence of depression is, depending on the estimate, three to ten times greater.

So far, just trends. But there are correlations in the data, too. Married people are happier and healthier than divorced or unmarried people. People are more likely to stay married if they are religious, well-educated, grew up in a two-parent home, married after age 20, and married as virgins. Compared with married couples, cohabiting couples enjoy sex less, are more often unfaithful, and (if they eventually marry) are more likely to divorce.

And then there's the root of (not all, but much) developmental evil: father-absence. Seven out of ten delinquents are from father-absent homes. Teenage boys from such homes are three times as likely to be incarcerated by age 30; for each additional year spent in a home without two parents, the risk of incarceration increases by 5%. Children from single-parent homes are more likely to be abused, to drop out of school, and (by a factor of five) to be poor. The presence of step-parents improves the numbers a little, but not much. Overall, the non-marital birth rate predicts a society's violent crime rate with striking accuracy.

Even the most expertly parsed data are not self-interpreting, of course. Myers and Lane have rather different interpretive styles: the former analytical and hortatory, very ready to propose voluntary or legislative remedies; the latter abstract and analytical, rarely venturing more than a tentative suggestion. Myers, a social psychologist, emphasizes culture and values; Lane, a political scientist, emphasizes institutions and systems.

Both emphasize that poverty is not the prime cause of our "social recession." Myers forcefully criticizes economic inequality in contemporary America, advocating increased progressivity and a ceiling on executive compensation. More cautiously, Lane concludes that "by increasing unemployment to control inflation we are apparently increasing misery for no direct (though possibly some indirect) gain in well-being." For the most part, however, both books are less concerned with injustice or exploitation than with individualism and its unintended consequences.

The most obvious of these is marital instability. Myers quotes the historian Lawrence Stone: "The scale of marital breakdown in the West since 1960 has no historical precedent. . . . There has been nothing like it for the last 2000 years, and probably longer." *The American Paradox* thoroughly documents the effects of this change and offers many sensible suggestions for coping with it, such as mandating parental leave and flextime, indexing the dependent exemption to inflation, adjusting tax rates on married couples' income, reforming divorce laws, automating child-support payments, and directly subsidizing two-parent families in various ways. It also makes a plausible, nonsectarian case for teaching virtue in the public schools.

As for the causes of the marriage crisis, Myers wisely recognizes that they go beyond mere selfishness or shallow ideals of "personal growth" to include urbanization and the disappearance of neighborhoods, the changing nature of work and the resulting economic progress of women, the declining efficacy of religious sanctions, the sexualization of advertising and entertainment, and of course, the wider availability of contraceptive technology. Individualism stands upon a vast historical scaffolding.

Lane describes a different portion of this scaffolding. In a long and subtle analysis of the incentive structure of market culture, he shows that the main sources of happiness ("intrinsic work enjoyment, family solidarity, social inclusion, sociability at the workplace") and unhappiness (chronic financial insecurity, overwork, etc.) are "externalities": matters respecting which markets are, in their normal workings, indifferent.

"It does not pay," he concludes, "to devote resources to benefits accruing to workers but not to the firm's net income."

The consequences of all this elicit from Lane a rare burst of eloquence. "There is a kind of famine of warm interpersonal relations, of easy-to-reach neighbors, of encircling, inclusive memberships, and of solidary family life . . . For people lacking in social support of this kind, unemployment has more serious effects, illnesses are more deadly, disappointment with one's children is harder to bear, bouts of depression last longer, and frustration and failed expectations of all kinds are more traumatic." Valuing intimacy more, income and power less, would counter this "loss of happiness." But how to bring that about—how to promote companionship rather than economic growth or procedural equality as a societal norm? Lane is chary of suggestions, pleading only that other social scientists give the matter more attention.

Statistically, the social recession has leveled off since the mid-1990s, though it's not clear why. What are our long-term prospects? Not everyone gracefully outlives his or her growing pains; some adolescents do go haywire, after all. It doesn't seem altogether impossible that humankind—or at any rate, American society—will go haywire. Not convulsively, perhaps, but just drifting into a psychic minimalism. Michael Walzer has imagined the nightmarish result of "individualism with a vengeance" and of an equally untrammeled skepticism and hedonism: "a human being thoroughly divorced, freed of parents, spouse, and children, watching pornographic performances in some dark theater, joining (it may be his only membership) this or that odd cult, which he will probably leave in a month or two for one still odder . . . dissociated, passive, lonely, ultimately featureless." This is not what emancipation was supposed to look like.

Doubt and freedom are sacred to us since the Enlightenment, and rightly. Whatever bonds and beliefs we hope to ground community on must be able to withstand all criticisms and temptations. But are there any such grounds? Myers recommends a nondoctrinaire theism ("leaving theologians and atheists to duke it out over the ancient what-is-truth question . . ."), but it is practically contentless. Lane looks wistfully to social science for "a better theory of measured (and not just inferred) utility." That sounds to me like a straw in the hurricane of consumer marketing and global competition.

Let's hope for a prophet. As it happens, my favorite prophet, D. H. Lawrence, has some apposite words. "Man has a double set of desires, the shallow and the profound, the personal, superficial, temporary desires, and the inner, impersonal, great desires that are fulfilled in long periods of time. The desires of the moment are easy to recognize, but the other ones, the deeper ones, are difficult. It is the business of our Chief Thinkers to tell us of our deeper desires, not to keep shrilling our little desires in our ears."

Myers and Lane (along with the late Christopher Lasch, another great 20th-century prophet) have done what Chief Thinkers ought to do. But when one contemplates the multitude of opposing voices—the market, TV and the movies, popular music, the advertising industry and, increasingly, the Internet—all ceaselessly shrilling our little desires in our ears, it's hard to be optimistic.

Why Be Moral?

As every parent knows, sometimes the only answer to "Why?" is "Because I say so." For a long time that was, at least in form, the most common answer to every society's ultimate "why" question: "Why be moral?" And of course, for an even longer time that question rarely arose, which (as parents, again, will readily agree) greatly simplified matters.

From the moral point of view, modernity may be defined as the unwillingness of the many, and no longer only a privileged or heroic few, to take "Because I (we) say so" for an answer. This fateful recalcitrance has many sources. One was a lightening of the burdens of daily life, thanks to the agricultural innovations of the high and late Middle Ages and the trickle-down effect of growing trade. Another was the evolution and differentiation of nation-states and national churches. Another was the success of natural philosophy, later called "science," which made asking "why?" seem in general a more promising thing to do. Perhaps most significant was the creation of a labor market, which eventually forced at least one new and urgent "why" question on everyone: "Why get my daily bread in this way rather than some other?" The result of these various but related historical developments was (here a slight flourish of trumpets) the birth of the individual.

This has not been an unmixed blessing. It's hard being an individual. It entails many more choices than we had on the savannah two million years ago, where our genetic endowment mostly took shape. Since, from the physiological point of view, every choice is a stress, it is possible, at least in theory, to have too many choices. At a certain point, "Because I say so" begins to look like an adaptive strategy.

Nevertheless, the Pandora's box of modernity is wide open. The historical changes mentioned above are irreversible.

Individuality may yet evaporate in the postmodern electronic cyber-collective, but it will not sink back into the premodern organic mass. Individuality is our condition, and freedom is therefore our moral fate, especially here in America, where the four horsemen of modernity—abundance, pluralism, technology, and mobility—are most firmly in the saddle.

As Alan Wolfe puts it: "Americans have come to accept the relevance of individual freedom, not only in their economic life, but in their moral life as well. The defining characteristic of the moral philosophy of Americans can therefore be described as the principle of moral freedom. Moral freedom means that individuals should determine for themselves what it means to lead a good and virtuous life. Contemporary Americans find answers to the perennial questions asked by theologians and moral philosophers, not by conforming to strictures handed down by God or nature, but by considering who they are, what others require, and what consequences follow from acting in one way rather than another."

What this means in practice is the subject of Wolfe's short but fascinating new book.* As in his last book, *One Nation, After All*, Wolfe and his associates interviewed approximately two hundred people in eight communities around the country; and once again he has fashioned the results into a seamless weave of narrative and interpretation, deftly alternating quotes and commentary. As before, he finds that by and large Americans are just trying to get by, good-humoredly but a little worriedly, in a world that's moving a bit too fast; eclectic, improvising, sometimes glancing wistfully at tradition and authority but always wary of them as well.

The organizing theme of the interviews was the meaning of virtue. Unsurprisingly, few of Wolfe's respondents had much to say about it in the abstract. Like most Americans on most subjects, they are uncomfortable with categorical statements. But

Moral Freedom: The Search for Virtue in a World of Choice by Alan Wolfe. Norton, 2001.

they were more forthcoming—positively chatty, it appears—when asked for their attitudes and feelings about individual virtues like loyalty, honesty, self-discipline, and forgiveness. The resulting slightly artificial intimacy and occasionally banal earnestness lends *Moral Freedom* some of the flavor of soap opera and talk radio, which are perhaps where many of those attitudes and feelings came from.

If Americans have a moral meta-principle, it is flexibility. "No absolutes" is our watchword. One might say (with apologies to Barry Goldwater): Extremism in the pursuit of virtue is no virtue; moderation in the practice of virtue is no vice. One owes loyalty to an employer or a spouse, but also to one's career and even one's own happiness. Honesty is the best policy, as long as it's reciprocated; and honesty toward big institutions (especially the IRS) doesn't really count. Self-discipline is essential to success, though pleasure is no less essential to emotional health. And so on, with the rule being: Adapt every rule to the circumstances. "Americans," Wolfe observes, "are consequentialists."

We have to be, he explains. For one thing, the old rule-givers no long command automatic deference. Even the Christians in his sample (a minority, and most of them apparently born-again rather than never-strayed) seem to rely on their own readings of Scripture, not authoritative institutional ones. And the stakes involved in moral judgment are different now. Traditional morality was "narrow but deep; the individual had few choices to make, but all those choices were serious." Present-day morality, by contrast, is "shallow but broad; we have many more moral issues to consider, even if few of them will result in eternal damnation, social ostracism, or the poorhouse."

Does this make for a certain moral squishiness? Wolfe, perhaps a tad too loyal to his respondents, denies it. It is true, he acknowledges, that Americans no longer "subject themselves to the severe and demanding tests of character imposed . . . by one version or another of the Protestant ethic." This does not mean, however, "that the morality by which people live now makes them soft. It means only that the new morality is different, making up in the bewildering array of temptations it must face what it lacks in vigor and unswerving self-confidence."

Sorry, but I'm afraid it sounds to me like we're soft. Certainly the extra-moral evidence points that way. Americans gobble junk food, watch TV, and guzzle gas without much restraint, as our waistlines and smog levels testify. We can't say no to tax loopholes or yes to taxes. We want military superiority but no casualties. Once a self-reliant nation of tinkerers and inventors, we now have little idea what makes our fancy gadgets tick. A man's word may once have been his bond, but now we lead the world in lawyers per capita. Aren't these character flaws? Wouldn't more "rigor" and less flexibility serve us well?

Until now, America's fabulous prosperity has blunted the force of such questions, and indeed made the whole issue of character somewhat moot. In our post-industrial (if that's what it is) capitalist society, most people's economic well-being does not seem dependent on other people's virtuous behavior. (Or even on one's own, for the fortunate minority enriched by the stock market or the financial casino.) Residential and commercial mobility make the behavior of individuals and businesses hard to monitor or sanction. Most of us are content to leave that to the experts anyway: the professional regulators, litigators, journalists, educators, and therapists who, in effect, administer our public morality—and who do so, for the most part, without reference to "virtue" or "character."

Two other recent developments seem particularly to cut against the psychic stability and coherence that are the foundation of character. The first, mentioned by Wolfe but more fully explored by Richard Sennett in *The Corrosion of Character*, is the altered shape and rhythm of careers. We change jobs and even livelihoods today with unprecedented frequency; and companies, too, disappear or metamorphose rapidly. In these circumstances, adaptability and detachment are at a premium, strong ties and long-term commitments at a discount.

More subtly but perhaps more fundamentally, television

and the Internet erode our capacity for inwardness. The sheer volume of stimuli, their velocity and decibel level, our passivity (except for an index finger on the mouse or the remote)—psychologically, these and other features of the "electronic millennium" (Sven Birkerts' phrase) add up to a new evolutionary niche. Our attention becomes more diffuse, shallow, and restless. Continuity is part of the very definition of character; and continuity is gradually but inexorably fraying, within us and without.

Wolfe's respondents are aware, at least peripherally, of these environmental changes, but are on the whole resigned to them. "The world is an incredibly dynamic place. Nothing stays the same," a Silicon Valley entrepreneur asserts in a tone of finality. They are, however, uneasy about the decline of religious belief. This is not, apparently, because Christian or non-Christian religious beliefs are true, but because they're useful. Like most conservative social critics, these ordinary people praise religion but decline to argue it. They want the socializing effects of authoritative worldviews for their children, provided the kids grow out of those views at the appropriate time, and not too painfully. As Wolfe puts it, cogently: "It is as if they want some of the practice of old-time character formation—especially a greater respect for order and discipline—without the rest of old-time character formation, especially theological instruction and an emphasis on religious obedience."

How entirely reasonable! But is it possible? Wolfe, impressed by his subjects' cheerful, humane pragmatism, seems to think so. But some of his readers will feel that the notion of "moral freedom" harbors, if not a contradiction, then at least a tension that might, and perhaps ought, to have made *Moral Freedom* a darker, more pessimistic book.

Enough . . . for Now

Until lately I thought the most troubling book I had ever read was *The End of Nature*, Bill McKibben's searching meditation on humankind's definitive eclipse of our nonhuman context. That book was not primarily a catalogue of likely environmental disasters, imminent or eventual, though there was more than enough of such worrisome news. What mainly preoccupied McKibben was that we have, without forethought, passed a momentous limit. By the end of the 20th century, the scale of human activity had grown so rapidly and enormously that the nonhuman world now exists on our sufferance—not this or that niche, but the character of the whole.

The resulting loss, McKibben suggested, cannot be gauged. In the last two centuries we Americans have destroyed many of the wonders of the world: the Colorado River and many of its sublime canyons (very nearly including the Grand Canyon), the California redwoods, the tall-grass prairie, the bison herds, the grizzlies. Each disappearance has occasioned much anguish among those who loved those places and creatures, at least in imagination. But in each case the idea of nature survived: our confidence, however thoughtless, that we might disfigure the planet here or there but could never overwhelm it; that we might misuse it, or even use up this or that aspect of it, but that as a whole it would endure, essentially as it always had, mute, unmasterable, sovereign in its indifference to us.

No longer. The increase of carbon dioxide and other "greenhouse" gases in the atmosphere, and the associated long-term climate changes, are capable of altering the distribution of life forms on earth so profoundly that the distinction between natural and artificial is imperiled. If "natural" means what happens without human intervention, outside human control, then the natural world has, in effect, disappeared. Even if global industrial activity is henceforth curtailed, which is hardly likely, we have already gone too far. We may yet avoid ruining the world, but we have already shrunk it drastically, with unpredictable—and probably not very healthy—effects on our collective psyche.

McKibben's next book, *Hope, Human and Wild*, reported on some comparatively sane ways of living within this shrunken world. It described the resourceful city administration of Curitiba, Brazil, with its ingenious low-tech solutions to flood control, garbage collection, and public transportation; the Indian district of Kerala, comparable to the United States in literacy and life expectancy with only one-seventieth the per-capita income; and, surprisingly, the northeastern U.S., where forests and wildlife have made an unexpected recovery in recent decades and communities have begun to defend themselves against industrial predation. Whether enough people will decide soon enough, as McKibben urged his readers, "to slow down, to reduce expectations, to undevelop" is highly uncertain. Still, the book left one with a chastened, tentative hopefulness about nature's prospects.

About the human prospect, however, it is hard to feel anything but terrified after reading *Enough: Staying Human in an Engineered Age.** As most people know, the genetic modification of many plants and animals—not by traditional crossbreeding but by directly inserting or altering individual genes—has been attempted, with much controversy about the results. According to one eminent scientist (James Watson, who discovered the structure of DNA), we are "at the beginning of a great GM [genetically modified] plant revolution," which will "ensure that crops contain a fuller array of nutrients . . . hold the key to distributing orally administered vaccine proteins . . . [and] provide ways as yet unimagined to preserve the environment." According to another (Harvard professor Richard Lewontin), the new technology merely "provides a powerful

*Times Books, 2004.

tool for the control of agricultural production by monopolistic producers of the inputs into agriculture, with no ultimate advantage either to farmers or consumers and with the possibility of destroying entire national agricultural economies."

An even more fateful controversy is just getting under way. It looks, many scientists claim, more and more likely that humans too can be genetically modified by such means, whether to prevent disease or to enhance desired traits. Some diseases, like cystic fibrosis, sickle-cell anemia, and Tay-Sachs disease, require the presence of a single defective gene. If a couple conceives several embryos in vitro, one without the disease-carrying gene can be chosen and implanted in the mother's womb. Such genetic screening is already available and is not particularly controversial.

But what if genes for IQ, physique, memory, musicality, etc. can be isolated and modified? What if a future child's character and personality can, to an initially limited but slowly increasing extent, be predetermined? Would such genetic interventions be morally right? And even if most people believe they wouldn't be, should they nevertheless be legal for those who believe otherwise?

Before approaching these questions, a factual caveat. Some scientists object that it does *not* look very likely that human behavior can be genetically modified. Steven Pinker, for example, writes that "not only is genetic enhancement not inevitable, it is not particularly likely in our lifetimes. . . . The human brain is not a bag of traits with one gene for each trait. Neural development is a staggeringly complex process guided by many genes interacting in feedback loops." Richard Lewontin likens the genetic code to a complex ecosystem: "You can always intervene and change something . . . but there's no knowing what the downstream effects will be or how it will affect the environment." Barry Commoner declares flatly: "By any reasonable measure, the findings [of the Human Genome Project] . . . destroy the scientific foundation of genetic engineering."

Still, it seems wise to consider ahead of time what we should do if genetic enhancement turns out to be feasible. If we are to pass this even more momentous limit, to alter human nature as we have always known it, let us at least not do so without forethought. And so: even if someday we can safely intervene in the biological mechanism of inheritance and get the results we want, ought we to do it? *Enough* is McKibben's answer, an unequivocal no.

In the first place, genetic enhancement is un-American. The essence of Americanism is found in that bold and noble sentence from the Declaration of Independence: "All men are created equal." As with all great truths, precisely what this statement means has been disputed. But it has been sufficiently well understood throughout the last two centuries to serve as the foundation of equality before the law and the basis of American democracy, which is perhaps humankind's grandest (however imperfect) political achievement.

Whatever "all men are created equal" may mean, exactly, it will no longer be true after a few dozen or a few hundred generations of genetic enhancement. As McKibben points out, like most technological advances in an already drastically unequal society, "designer" genes would benefit the rich far more than the poor:

> They would take the gap in power, wealth, and education that currently divides both our society and the world at large, and write that division into our very biology. A sixth of the American population lacks health insurance of any kind—they can't afford to go to the doctor for a *checkup*. And much of the rest of the world is far worse off. If we can't afford the fifty cents a person it would take to buy bed nets to protect most of Africa from malaria, it is unlikely we will extend to anyone but the top tax bracket these latest forms of genetic technology.

These are not mere Luddite mutterings. According to Princeton geneticist Lee Silver, a prominent advocate of the new technology, "emotional stability, long-term happiness, inborn talents, increased creativity, healthy bodies—these could be the starting points chosen for the children of the rich," while "obesity, heart disease, hypertension, alcoholism, mental illness—these will be the diseases left to drift randomly among the families of the underclass." The "GenRich" (i.e., genetically enhanced) minority, Silver continues, will control "all aspects of the economy, the media, the entertainment industry, and the knowledge industry." Eventually, "the GenRich class and the Natural class [i.e., the rest of us] will become . . . entirely separate species with no ability to crossbreed, and with as much romantic interest in each other as a current human would have for a chimpanzee."

Though Silver and other techno-libertarians are perfectly happy with this prospect, I call it un-American. As if to explicate the Declaration of Independence, Thomas Jefferson, its principal author, later wrote: "The general spread of the light of science has already laid open to every view the palpable truth, that the mass of mankind has not been born with saddles on their backs, nor a favored few booted and spurred, ready to ride them legitimately, by the grace of God." But one must ask, what science once gave, is science now about to take away? "The ultimate question raised by biotechnology," concludes Francis Fukuyama in his very astute *Our Posthuman Future*, is: "What will happen to political rights once we are able to, in effect, breed some people with saddles on their backs, and others with boots and spurs?" What will happen, pretty clearly, is the end of democracy and the American ideal. A modest proposal, therefore: shouldn't we get a little closer to attaining those things before we risk losing them forever merely in order that a privileged minority can ascend to superhumanity (and, not incidentally, so that a powerful industry can reap enormous profits)?

But this is to assume, perhaps foolishly, that we will have some choice in the matter. Perhaps we won't. "Whether we like it or not," Lee Silver admonishes, "the global marketplace will reign supreme." There you have it—the antagonism between democratic deliberation and free-market fundamentalism could not be more forthrightly, even contemptuously, expressed. There's a lot of money to be made in biotech, as there was in generating greenhouse gases, even if those activities turn our inner and outer worlds upside down. Case closed. Get over it.

The political argument for waiting is straightforward and, it seems to me, unanswerable. But most of *Enough* is devoted to making a deeper, more ambitious, more difficult argument against human genetic engineering: an argument from meaning. The promise of the new technologies (McKibben also discusses robotics and nanotechnology, the use of molecules for computing, manufacturing, etc.) is fabulous. Newly formulated gene packages will improve our every physical, emotional, and intellectual capability, eventually without limit. Beginning with the more directly gene-dependent ones, every disease will be eradicated, including cancer—even including aging: immortality too is part of the program. Nanobots (contingents of molecule-size robots) with unimaginable information-processing capacity will synthesize food, assemble consumer goods, and clean up waste, thereby eliminating hunger, poverty, and pollution. And in the fullness of time, they will construct a vastly superior species, thereby eliminating us.

Some of these, as McKibben shows, are false promises. To take a longstanding one: the Green Revolution in agriculture has, it is true, invariably increased plant yields, but it has also invariably increased micronutrient deficiencies and small-farmer indebtedness as well. The latest genetically engineered miracle, "golden rice," is a will-of-the-wisp. Biotechnology is not the solution to world hunger; biodiversity is. Low-tech solutions are also readily available for Third World poverty and disease; though since they are less profitable than high-tech solutions, they require a little disinterested First World support. The brand-new promise of nanotechnology is also dubious, even if feasible: nanoweapons, or even nano-accidents, would be far more devastating than present-day biological or chemical weapons.

But whether feasible or not, post-humanity is, McKibben argues, a poisoned gift as long as we have not yet achieved humanity. All the proposed new technologies aim at a fundamentally similar result: more. They aim to make our genetic hardware, our resources, our actions in some way larger or faster or easier. More computational power or muscle mass or dexterity or serotonin or orgasmic potency; faster communication or transportation or food preparation; easier work or no work. More lifespan, sensory inputs, entertainments, et cetera ad infinitum. More and faster and easier are not, in general, bad. On the contrary, they are, other things being equal, good. But sometimes—as in the near future, perhaps, when a flood of new stimuli and experiences may overwhelm our sensory and imaginative capacity to assimilate them, not to mention our political capacity to keep them from rending humankind's already precarious community—the good can be the enemy of the best.

What then, if not more, is best for human beings now? McKibben bravely faces this all-important question and throws out some fruitful hints. He cites some fascinating psychological research on joy, in particular the "almost trance-like state" the subjects entered when their work was going especially well. In this state, "fatigue, hunger, or discomfort ceased to matter." This ecstatic experience seems to derive from "the intense concentration that risk and adversity entail"; it "arises more from sensory focus than sensory overload"—from going inward, that is, rather than simply adding on, whether data, circuits, or genes. The world, as research subjects testify in a striking formulation, "falls away." This sounds a good deal like the peak experiences described by mystics and meditators. It also bears some resemblance to the "deep time" of fully engaged reading, evoked memorably by literary critic Sven Birkerts in *The Gutenberg Elegies*. It even (or so it seems to me) remotely echoes Nietzsche's enigmatic allusions to "self-overcoming."

McKibben's point is that there's an inner world as well as an outer world, and penetrating the one may be as essential to human fulfillment as conquering the other. The new hypertechnologies will facilitate the latter but not the former. Since our inclination is usually to evade what's difficult, we may find an increasing disproportion between our power and our depth. If there really is, as he speculates, a "strange connection between effort and joy and pride and reward," then perhaps limitless abundance would be less satisfying than the techno-utopians suppose.

It is perfectly true, of course, that inwardness—or self-cultivation or self-overcoming or whatever you like to call it—requires a sufficiency of material goods. Underfed and over-worked people should not be asked to forego further calories or conveniences. But as McKibben tirelessly reiterates, we in the developed world are already pretty close to the "enough" point. "We have reached a point of great comfort and ease relative to the past. The real question is whether, having reached that point, we want to trade it in for something essentially unknown." Turning back technologically, or even standing still, is no more desirable than it is possible. But it's at least thinkable that "the rush of technological innovation that's marked the last five hundred years can finally slow, and spread out to water the whole delta of human possibility." And to begin, for decency's sake, with those who are now much farther from the "enough" point than we are would provide a pretty challenging technological agenda for the rest of this century, at least.

A tiny reservation: heartily as I agree with McKibben, I am tempted to amend his battle-cry to "Enough . . . for now." We can't really know, after all, how a grown-up human race would regard this question. Perhaps someday in the distant future we will want, as a species, to assume a new form of life. Perhaps we will have together come to fruit, reached an unsurpass-able ripeness, a stable equipoise of individuality and community, solidarity and self-assertion, such that nowhere on earth remain large pools of unnecessary pain or ignorance, such that all or most possible harmonies within us and among us have been sounded and danced to. Then, not from fear that one's future child may be left behind in a hectic competition for top pre-schools, or from any such desperately sad and banal motive, but instead with a grateful reverence for the rounded humanity and exquisite comity we will by then have perfected together, some may volunteer to renounce that perfection and be tinkered with.

If that's how it happens, then so be it. But we today should leave to those who will be, by our own lights and through our own efforts, wiser than us, a decision that is beyond our present wisdom. We should, for the future's sake, acknowledge the limits of our wisdom. We are not wise enough—not now, not for a long time—to justify abdicating our specieshood, renouncing our humanity forever in favor of post-humanity. We are wise enough, though, to make a good life for our species now and to see a few steps in the direction of a better one.

At least, I hope we are. We will be, at any rate, if we can learn from Bill McKibben's humane and far-seeing book.

Shipwrecked

When D. H. Lawrence died in 1930, E. M. Forster, protesting the generally obtuse and malicious obituary notices, wrote that he was "the greatest imaginative novelist of his generation"— a generation that included Proust, Joyce, Kafka, and Mann. Not many critics nowadays would go that far; still, Lawrence's standing as a major novelist seems secure.

The opposite is true of his reputation as a thinker. Lawrence wrote a great deal about politics, psychology, sexuality, and religion (most of it collected in the two volumes of *Phoenix: The Posthumous Papers*). Insofar as his ideas on these subjects have been considered at all, it has usually been as a shadowy backdrop to the fiction. Lawrence's portraits of birds, beasts, and flowers, of rural life, of the growth of individual consciousness, and of the relations between modern men and women— these are widely acclaimed. But his ideas are just an embarrassment. Bertrand Russell wrote that Lawrence had "developed the whole philosophy of fascism before the politicians had thought of it." Kate Millett in *Sexual Politics* labeled him "the most talented and fervid" of "counterrevolutionary sexual politicians." According to Philip Rahv, "in the political sphere . . . he was a fantast, pure and simple." Susan Sontag dismissed his notions about sexuality as "reactionary" and "marred by class romanticism." And so it goes: praise for Lawrence the artist, but for Lawrence the prophet, contempt or, at best, tactful neglect.

Every critical consensus contains a measure of truth. Lawrence said a great many foolish things, and there is no point in glossing over them. But there is not much point, either, in dwelling on them—as though his ideas ever had some sort of influence or prestige, which urgently needs to be countered. Like Nietzsche, whom he resembles in astonishingly many ways, Lawrence tried to diagnose and oppose an entire civilization, his and ours. He was defeated, even routed. But the attempt deserves more sympathetic attention than it has received. Karl Jaspers lauded Kierkegaard and Nietzsche for having "dared to be shipwrecked": "They are so to speak, representative destinies, sacrifices whose way out of the world leads to experiences for others. . . . Through them we have intimations of something we could never have perceived without such sacrifices, of something that seems essential, which even today we cannot adequately grasp." To many who are ambivalent about modernity, Lawrence also revealed something that even today "we cannot adequately grasp," but which nonetheless "seems essential"; and if he often made a fool of himself in the process, it was an indispensable, even a heroic, folly.

Lawrence's starting point was the same problem that had confronted Kierkegaard and Nietzsche: nihilism, or the "death of God." The modern age, beginning with the Enlightenment, had seemed to promise a complete liberation from traditional dogmas. Previously unquestioned loyalties—religious, political, racial, familial—were eroded by the spread of philosophical materialism and ethical individualism. But since then, a question has gradually dawned in those countries where modernity has taken root: If the beliefs that formerly made life seem worth living—beliefs about God, political authority, racial uniqueness, and sexual destiny—are seen to be illusions, then what *does* make life worth living?

That question is dramatized memorably in John Stuart Mill's *Autobiography*. The young Mill fell into an intense depression because he had no sustaining illusions—or, as he put it, because "the habit of analysis tends to wear away the feelings." It is hard to think of two figures more different than Mill and Lawrence, yet this pithy and poignant phrase of Mill's exactly expresses Lawrence's sense of the modern predicament. Like so many nineteenth-century thinkers, Mill had discovered that criticism could liberate but not motivate. There were plenty of traditional dogmas left to criticize in his time, so he kept at criticism and made an honorable career of it. But things were different for Lawrence.

It may be difficult nowadays to appreciate just how enlightened early twentieth-century England was, at least compared with twenty-first-century America. Intellectual and moral emancipation were very widely diffused—the prosperity and stability of the Victorian age had produced an extraordinary cultural flowering. As regards anything that deserves to be called liberation, Ursula Brangwen, Lawrence's most notable heroine, was miles ahead of most contemporary feminists; and the same relation holds between her counterpart, Rupert Birkin, and even the most egalitarian contemporary male. Both are, like most of Lawrence's protagonists, like Lawrence himself, aiming neither to defy traditional values nor to resurrect them, but rather to imagine a way of life that takes their disappearance for granted.

So much has been written about Lawrence's "neo-primitivism" and "nostalgia" that it seems worth stressing how far in advance he was of most present-day progressives, at least in one respect. He saw all the way to the end of modern emancipation; and though he sometimes cursed it, he never expected, or even hoped, that we could avoid it. All he wanted was that we survive it. One of his most striking statements about the modern dilemma occurs in the unpublished prologue to *Women in Love*:

> But if there *be* no great philosophic idea, if, for the time being, mankind, instead of going through a period of growth, is going through a corresponding process of decay and decomposition from some old, fulfilled, obsolete idea, then what is the good of educating? Decay and decomposition will take their own way. It is impossible to educate for this end, impossible to teach the world how to die away from its achieved, nullified form. The autumn must take place in every individual soul, as well as in all the people; all must die, individually and socially. Education is a process of striving to a new, unanimous being, a whole organic form. But when winter has set in, when the frosts are strangling the leaves off the trees and the birds are

silent knots of darkness, how can there be a unanimous movement towards a whole summer of florescence? There can be
none of this, only submission to the death of this nature, in the
winter that has come upon mankind, and a cherishing of the
unknown that is unknown for many a day yet, buds that may not
open till a far off season comes, when the season of death has
passed away.

This is only a vast and vague intuition, not a fully worked-out
philosophy of history. Clearly, though, it is not a lament for
the pre-modern order or a call to reconstruct it. And whatever
the coming "unknown" may turn out to be, the "old, fulfilled,
obsolete idea" that we must, according to Lawrence, "die away"
from certainly includes political and sexual subjection.

It also, however, includes—and here is the source of Lawrence's doubtful contemporary reputation—their negation:
political and sexual equality, mechanically defined. Lawrence
criticized equality as an ideal. But not because he wanted property and power to be distributed unequally. He wanted them
abolished or, better, outgrown. For capitalist and patriarchal
ideology he had only contempt. For socialist and feminist ideology he had instead fraternal impatience, precisely because they
seemed to have no higher end in view than more property and
power for their constituencies. The undeniable justice of this
demand did not, he believed, make it any less a dead end.

Lawrence's poems and essays are full of furious invective
against the dominion of money. "The whole great form of our
era will have to go," he declared; and he left no doubt that this
meant, among other things, private ownership of the means of
production. Yet he could also write: "I know that we had all
better hang ourselves at once than enter on a struggle which
shall be a fight for the ownership or non-ownership of property, pure and simple, and nothing more." He meant that a new
form of ownership is not necessarily a new form of life, and that
to live and work in a mass is the death of individuality, even if
the mass is well fed. Although Lawrence has been condemned
as an authoritarian for saying such things, I think they are just

about what William Blake or William Morris would have said (perhaps a touch less stridently) if confronted with twentieth-century social democracy.

The case of feminism is more complicated. Lawrence wrote some staggeringly wrongheaded things on this subject, and some wise things. I suspect that when he contemplated the sexual future, he saw Bloomsbury writ large—which meant, to him, the triumph of androgyny as an ideal. That was deepest anathema, for though Lawrence's lifework is a landmark in the demystification of sex, it is also a monument to the mystery of sex, which must disappear, he thought, from an androgynous world. Rilke—whom no one has ever been foolish enough to label a counterrevolutionary sexual politician—included in his *Letters to a Young Poet* several stirring passages on sexual equality but also this cautionary comment: "The girl and the woman, in their new, their own unfolding, will but in passing be imitators of masculine ways, good and bad, and repeaters of masculine professions. After the uncertainty of such transitions it will become apparent that women were only going through the profusion and the vicissitude of those (often ridiculous) disguises in order to cleanse their own most characteristic nature of the distorting influences of the other sex." Lawrence devoted much passionate writing to elaborating kindred insights. They are complex insights, and cost him a great many trials and some appalling errors. But it was a post-revolutionary, not a pre-revolutionary, world that Lawrence, like Rilke, was trying to envisage.

Just what sort of world Lawrence had in mind is difficult to know. He was a prophet without a program, not only because he died too soon but also because it's hard to be explicit about primal realities. He believed that the universe and the individual soul were pulsing with mysteries, from which men and women were perennially distracted by want or greed or dogma. Income redistribution and affirmative action were necessary preliminaries, to clear away the distractions; but if they became ends in themselves, then the last state of humankind would be worse than the first. He thought that beauty, graceful physical movement, unselfconscious emotional directness, and a sense, even an inarticulate sense, of connection to the cosmos, however defined—to the sun, to the wilderness, to the rhythms of a craft or the rites of a tribe—were organic necessities of a sane human life. He thought that reason was not something fundamental to human identity but rather a phenomenon of the surface: "I conceive a man's body as a kind of flame . . . and the intellect is just the light that is shed on the things around." He thought that every free spirit revered someone or something braver or finer than itself, and that this spontaneous reverence was the basis of any viable social order. "Man has little needs and deeper needs," he wrote; and he complained that the workers' and women's movements of his time spoke chiefly to our little needs and could therefore lead only to universal mediocrity and frustration.

Lawrence did not despise socialism or feminism, but he despaired of them. It is this despair that accounts for his frequent, complementary excesses of bitterness and sentimentality. He had so few comrades, and such urgent intimations of catastrophe. "We have fallen into the mistake of living from our little needs till we have almost lost our deeper needs in a sort of madness." Whether or not you accept Lawrence's conception of our deeper needs, it is hard to deny the madness. "A wave of generosity or a wave of death," he prophesied, shortly before his own death. We know which came to pass.

Like all the other great diagnosticians of nihilism, Lawrence recognized that although the irrational cannot survive, the rational does not suffice. We live, he taught, by mysterious influxes of spirit, of what Blake called "Energy." Irrationalists make superstitions out of these mysteries, rationalists make systems, each in a futile, anxious attempt at mastery. Lawrence wanted us to submit: to give up the characteristic modern forms—possessive individualism, technological messianism, political and sexual *ressentiment*—of humankind's chronic pretense at mastery. But since that sort of submission is more delicate and difficult than self-assertion, he mainly succeeded in provoking misunderstanding or abuse.

Perhaps only other inspired fools can take his measure. In *The Prisoner of Sex*, Norman Mailer paid Lawrence this exquisite and definitive tribute: "What he was asking for had been too hard for him, it is more than hard for us; his life was, yes, a torture, and we draw back in fear, for we would not know how to try to burn by such a light."

The Humanity of Women

Philip Larkin wryly wrote:

> Sexual intercourse began
> In nineteen-sixty-three,
> Between the end of the Chatterly ban
> And the Beatles' first LP.

Actually, as far as women are concerned, that's just about right, according to Barbara Ehrenreich, Elizabeth Hess, and Gloria Jacobs*. Since around 1960, the number of women who have lived, or at least aspired to live, their sexual lives on something approaching their own terms has grown from a daring minority to a respectable majority. This is, by any historical standard, a revolution; and like most revolutions, it's been hotly contested. Part of the conservative backlash against feminism has been an effort to minimize this achievement, to portray women's sexual liberation as a joke or a failure or a danger. Even among some feminists there has been a retreat, or at least a revaluation. Now is the time, Ehrenreich *et al.* have decided, to speak up for sex— to set down a preliminary record of women's advance, on the principle that "a victory, no matter how partial or unfinished, is worth little until it has been acknowledged." *Re-Making Love* is full of fascinating social history and invaluable social criticism. It's a witty, entertaining, but also urgent book, a reminder that we've come a long way—women and men both—and an invitation to go all the way, from sexual emancipation to political and economic equality.

The sexual revolution was made possible by America's postwar prosperity, which had two far-reaching effects: it put vast

---

Re-Making Love: The Feminization of Sex by Barbara Ehrenreich, Elizabeth Hess, and Gloria Jacobs. Anchor Press/Doubleday, 1986.

purchasing power into the hands of adolescents, and it provided jobs and apartments in the cities for single women. The teen culture of the late 1950s and early 60s was, as Ehrenreich, Hess, and Jacobs describe it, a bleak, conformist affair, which burdened girls with the obligation both to attract boys and to fend them off. Then came Beatlemania—the first mass outburst of female libido. The Beatles themselves were not initially sexual rebels, but there were several subversive aspects to the excitement they generated. For one thing, there was a hint of gender ambiguity about them: the long hair, the high-pitched harmonies, the playful silliness. They could not have been more different from the inarticulate jocks with crewcuts who were pawing high-school girls at date's end all across America. Even more important, the Beatles were, in a sense, the creation of their female fans, without whom they would have languished in the obscurity of working-class Liverpool. The very fact that nobody could hear a note of music at their concerts suggests that the crowd was really intoxicated with its own power. That may have been, the authors speculate, the real meaning of Beatlemania: a first, inchoate expression of female power, the opening salvo of the sexual revolution.

In any case, the main battles—or rather, millions of local skirmishes—followed soon. In the sexual-advice literature of the 1940s and 50s, male dominance and female passivity were presented as virtually a law of nature. Here's a typical quote from a classic marriage manual of the period:

> For the male, sex involves an objective act of his doing, but for the female it does not. . . . her role is passive. It is not as easy as rolling off a log for her. It is easier. It is as easy as being the log itself.

These quaint notions were put to rout by a dizzying succession of sexual manifestoes, including *Sex and the Single Girl* (1962), *The Feminine Mystique* (1963), Jacqueline Susann's pulp novel *Valley of the Dolls* (1966), Masters and Johnson's *Human Sexual Response* (1966), and *The Sensuous Woman* (1969). Behind them all, the authors claim, were the landmark Kinsey Reports, whose emphasis on orgasms taught Americans to think quantitatively about sex. Before Kinsey, what women were supposed to expect from sex was described as "satisfaction" or "fulfillment"—pretty obvious euphemisms designed to disguise the fact that more than 50 per cent of American women rarely or never had orgasms. Kinsey made verbal evasion more difficult. One after another, first in discourse and then in deed, the redoubts of sexual reticence fell: masturbation, oral sex, anal sex, same-sex sex, erotic paraphernalia, sadomasochism, the lush, secret garden of sexual fantasy. Most of the new talking and doing came from women, impatient to disavow immemorial patterns of unsatisfying sex and find out what might be better. The whole glorious quest, sometimes quixotic, sometimes heroic, is chronicled in *Re-Making Love*.

The quest led into some curious byways. "Desire takes strange paths through a landscape of inequality," the authors write. They're well aware that consumer culture can co-opt and distort even the most unruly passions. When radical innovation collides with established power, like an irresistible force meeting an immovable object, the results are unpredictable. Who could have predicted suburban Tupperware-style parties featuring edible nighties, fruit-flavored erection and nipple creams, Rub-Her Bands, Lick-Ness Monsters, Orgy Butter, Vice Spice Pills, and Emotion Lotions?

Even more curious is the saga of fundamentalist sex. A chapter of *Re-Making Love* is devoted to the encounter between the Christian right and the sexual revolution. Surprisingly, it has not been an entirely hostile encounter. Marabel Morgan's bestselling book *The Total Woman,* with its numerous spinoffs and successors (including some startlingly explicit marriage manuals from fundamentalist ministers), clearly tapped into a reservoir of confusion and anxiety among religious women. The testimony of these women, for whom revolt was unthinkable and continued frustration unbearable, is among the most affecting things in *Re-Making Love*.

Ehrenreich, Hess, and Jacobs have a purpose in recounting all this history, apart from its piquancy. "In a society that holds an increasingly punitive work ethic above any ethic of love or compassion," they write, it's more important than ever "to assert *pleasure*—perhaps especially sexual pleasure—as a legitimate social goal." The current conservative attack on sexual freedom is not limited to the obvious targets: abortion, pornography, gay rights, sex education. It's also directed at welfare programs, day care funding, affirmative action, and comparable-worth legislation, and for much the same reason: fear of women's sexual autonomy. Sexual liberation was one aspect of a more expansive and generous sense of social possibilities; the attempt to roll it back is an integral part of Reaganism: austerity for the many, privilege for the few. The state-sponsored anti-feminist backlash is one more proof of the familiar feminist slogan: the personal is political.

Re-Making Love is a short book, and sex is a large subject. Naturally, some questions remain open. In particular, the question that haunts this and every discussion of sex is: what, if anything, does it mean? Is it a sublime drama of isolation and fusion, completion and depletion, self-assertion and self-abandonment? Or is it no more than the most exquisite of sensations? Is sex without romantic or symbolic meaning one-dimensional, exploitative, compulsive? Or conversely, is the need for meaning itself a neurotic compulsion, a symptom of physiological infirmity? Is the separation of sex and love one of the innumerable trivializing effects of consumer culture? Or a liberation from age-old patriarchal ideology?

Ehrenreich and her colleagues come down squarely, and perhaps a little too quickly, on one side of these questions. It is true, as they point out again and again, that the old romantic rhetoric, which celebrated a specific ideal of complementarity—male initiative and female response, male heroism and female nurture, male speech and female silence, male strength and female grace—was three-fourths, perhaps even nine-tenths, obfuscation. Constructed of lazy generalizations, and enforced with a compensating ferocity, that ideal has stunted inconceivably many women's—and men's—lives. The authors are unquestionably right to say: not that; never again.

But is it true that "sex should have no ultimate meaning other than pleasure, and no great mystery except how to achieve it"? The authors regularly invoke terms like "negotiation," "trade," and "work," and they remark, with apparent approval, that "if there is a single metaphor for the reconstructed heterosexuality of the seventies, it would be a bartering session." You'd think that Ehrenreich, perhaps our sharpest radical social critic, would be a bit more wary of commercial language. Sexual equality is, without a doubt, a quantitative matter—but exclusively so? Between mystique and marketplace, mightn't there be some other way to conceive of sex?

I confess I don't know, which seems to me another excellent reason for supporting the women's movement. Just as, in Hegel's famous master-slave dialectic, the master can never enjoy the certainty of uncoerced allegiance, so too we will never be sure what brings male and female bodies together as long as women are, by and large, economically dependent on men. Transcendence, affection, lust, reproductive instinct—these are hard enough to sort out. The added complication of economic insecurity, based on unequal power, distorts our experience beyond understanding.

Only a few pioneer spirits, like Whitman, Rilke, and Lawrence, have begun to imagine sex without power; and even they got no more than a glimpse. Eighty years ago Rilke, too, advocated "re-making love." His tone and emphasis differed slightly from those of some contemporary feminists, including Ehrenreich, Hess, and Jacobs. Yet only the victory of their movement can bring his extraordinarily beautiful vision to fulfillment:

> The humanity of woman, borne its full time in suffering and humiliation, will come to light when she will have stripped off the conventions of mere femininity in the mutations of her outward status, and those men who do not yet feel it approaching today will be surprised and struck by it. Some day . . . there will

be girls and women whose name will no longer signify merely an opposite of the masculine, but something in itself, something that makes one think, not of any complement and limit, but only of life and existence: the feminine human being.

This advance will (at first much against the will of the outstripped men) change the love-experience, which is now full of error, will alter it from the ground up, reshape it into a relation that is meant to be of one human being to another, no longer of man to woman. And this more human love, which will fulfill itself, infinitely considerate and gentle, and kind and clear in binding and releasing, will resemble that which we are preparing with struggle and toil: the love that consists in this, that two solitudes protect and border and salute each other.

Into the Dark?

In 1984 Ronald Reagan announced, with characteristic indifference to fact, that it was "morning in America." A quarter-century later, the twilight, then already perceptible, has deepened. The international financial position of the United States is ruinous. Globally, attitudes toward American policy range from misgiving to loathing. The foreseeable consequences of climate change and environmental pollution range from painful to catastrophic. For most Americans (especially the tens of millions without health insurance), medical care is the worst in any advanced industrial society. Economic insecurity is epidemic; overwork and high stress are the rule rather than the exception; inequality is at an all-time high; trust in government is at an all-time low (though perhaps not low enough). The (until recently) governing party openly aspires to permanent one-party rule and a Caesarist executive. Civic virtue, lately renamed "social capital," is waning; neighborliness has dwindled to the point of near-anomie. Functional illiteracy is rampant: in most non-affluent school districts, the public schools are not merely ineffectual but often unsafe as well. Nearly half of all Americans believe that the earth is 10,000 years old or less and that angels and other supernatural beings regularly intervene in terrestrial affairs. The average American's day includes six minutes playing sports, five minutes reading books, one minute making music, thirty seconds attending a play or concert, twenty-five seconds making or viewing art, and four hours watching television. And even Americans who don't watch television are perfused by a stream of commercial messages so intense and ubiquitous as to constitute a culture (in the biological as well as social sense) of consumption. Compared with the imagined noonday brilliance of that vibrant idyll, Walt Whitman's

Democratic Vistas, the prospects for contemporary American civilization are heartbreakingly bleak.

Morris Berman's *Dark Ages America** is one of the most important books published in recent years. It is a sequel to Berman's *The Twilight of American Culture* (2000), a shorter, more impressionistic book that persuasively evoked contemporary parallels to the collapse of Roman imperial civilization and suggested that, like the Greco-Roman heritage, Enlightenment ideals may survive the coming era of globalized barbarism underground, in quasi-monastic networks and communities.

Although the play of "twilight" and "dark" in the two books' titles implies forward (or backward) motion, *Dark Ages America* does not try to go beyond *The Twilight of American Culture* so much as beneath it. The earlier book was primarily descriptive; the new one is diagnostic as well. Berman is a distinguished historian of medieval and early modern culture, and he imports from his study of alchemy the maxim: "as above, so below." That is, the macrocosm and the microcosm—the visible dynamics of global political economy and the subtleties of culture and social psychology; grand strategy and the grain of everyday life—reflect and determine one another.

Thus, for example, the unrestricted movement of capital, the *ultima ratio* of American foreign and domestic policy, requires weak or corrupt—in any case, acquiescent—governments, since otherwise they might try to improve their bargaining position by combining with other governments and encouraging labor organization. Ineffectual governments and labor unions in turn require a weakening of impulses toward cooperation, solidarity, and citizen initiative. Very helpful toward this end is the redefinition of the good life as a life of continuous and increasing individual consumption—which, since it is a false definition, necessitates unremitting indoctrination by means of advertising. Expanding consumption in turn requires technological innovation, mass production, a population willing to

Dark Ages America: The Final Phase of Empire. Norton, 2006.

put up with insecure, regimented, and frequently stupefying work (the effects of which are assuaged by entertainments only a little more refined and wholesome than Roman circuses), and the exploitation of resources on a vast scale. And these requirements of expanding consumption in turn promote the concentration and mobility of capital. In Berman's apt formulation: "Global process, local fallout."

Whether or not the elites who profit by the degradation of culture and character intend these consequences, or even perceive them, is beside the point. Whatever anyone may intend, forms of life produce individuals adapted to them, just as physical environments do. "Civilizations are a package deal," Berman observes. Much of the value of *Dark Ages America* lies in tracing the adaptations and interdependencies implicit in the civilization we have evolved.

The ethos of American individualism is Berman's particular preoccupation. It has frontier roots but is also an effect (as well as a contributing cause) of the victory of automobiles and suburbanization over mass transit and European-style city planning. "The relentless American habit of choosing the individual solution over the collective one," Berman writes, underlies "the design of our cities, including the rise of a car culture, the growth of the suburbs, and the nature of our architecture, [which] has had an overwhelming impact on the life of the nation as a whole, reflecting back on all the issues discussed here: work, children, media, community, economy, technology, globalization, and, especially, US foreign policy. The physical arrangements of our lives mirror the spiritual ones."

American foreign policy all too clearly expresses this preference for "individual solutions over collective ones." The basic principle of world order—willingness to accept limits on national sovereignty in deference to international law and opinion—has always been unpopular in this country. As a result, American international behavior has been so highhanded that, even among normally sympathetic foreign elites, the US is widely regarded as a rogue nation and the chief threat to global peace and welfare. And individualism affects the substance as well as the style of US foreign policy. The culture of cars, suburbs, and shopping is resource-intensive, and in particular, energy-intensive. Control of global energy resources has therefore been the linchpin of US policy since World War II, as Berman shows.

As above, so below: the texture of daily life and the contours of individual psychology within a civilization are intimately related to its science and technology. In the first chapter of *Dark Ages America*, Berman elaborates a concept borrowed from the sociologist Zygmunt Bauman: "liquid modernity." This names a society "characterized by speed, fluidity, and transience . . . a permanent state of contingency." It's true that this acceleration has been underway since the Industrial Revolution and that Marx discoursed brilliantly on it in the *Communist Manifesto*. But the pace of social change has increased exponentially in the last few decades, thanks to both computer technology and the demise of the Bretton Woods international economic order, which freed capital to move around the world instantaneously. Along with all the blessings of electronic technology have come enormous, unprecedented stresses on our psyches and metabolisms. "Everything in contemporary society discourages inwardness," the literary critic Sven Birkerts has written. Berman illustrates copiously.

Dark Ages America is a synthesis. All the elements of Berman's critique have been made before, though they are assembled here with rare skill and comprehensiveness. What is perhaps most original is Berman's frank admission that he sees no way out. Indignation is usually followed by exhortation, but not in this book or its predecessor. It's not that Berman sees nothing valuable in contemporary American society and no one struggling against the trends he has identified. He simply doesn't hold out much hope for them. "In the process of decline a civilization may, from time to time, rally for a while; but it is the overall trajectory, the structural properties of the situation, that ultimately determine the outcome."

Just what form the new Dark Ages may take does not emerge from Berman's account. Contrary to fashionable demurrers, the Dark Ages were indeed dark: a half-millennium-long, nearly complete eclipse of reason, which classical culture barely and fortuitously survived. It is bound to be different this time around. Then, the imagination was starved; now it will be smothered: by commercial images, by ersatz sensations, by media babble, by corporate and governmental doublespeak. Still, we have at least learned a lot about information storage and retrieval. Maybe those skills will also prove useful for cultural survival.

It is not much easier to accept the death of one's culture than one's own death—perhaps it is even harder if one has had a happy life and known intellectual or aesthetic pleasure. That is why Berman wrote this book, though convinced of its futility. Thankfully, he cites a few lines from the ending of Gore Vidal's *Julian* that temper the pain a little:

> With Julian, the light went out, and now nothing remains but to let the darkness come, and hope for a new sun and another day, born of time's mystery and man's love of light.

Crowds and Culture

This spring* I spent two weeks in Italy. According to guide-books and friends, April should have been ideal: after the rains but before the summer heat and the tourist season. In the event, it rained every day, and the churches, museums, markets, gardens, ruins, and temples were thronged with tourists. Disappointment makes one philosophical, and since it's hard to philosophize for very long about the weather, I soon began to reflect on the crowds.

I had prepared for the trip by reading *Twilight in Italy* and *Sea and Sardinia* by D. H. Lawrence and *Old Calabria* by Norman Douglas. Lovely books and written, apparently, just before the Flood. Trains and boats were crowded in these books, but with Italians, not tourists (the authors traveled second- or third class). Cultural sites and picturesque scenery were not overrun, as they are now. Only artists and the upper or upper-middle classes either wanted to or could afford to visit; and as a result, those who came found what they were looking for. Unlike me.

In 1930 the Spanish philosopher Ortega y Gasset published *The Revolt of the Masses*, whose opening pages announced a momentous phenomenon, which he called "plenitude" but might equally well have called "crowdedness." For the first time in Europe, Ortega wrote,

> towns are full of people, houses full of tenants, hotels full of guests, trains full of travelers, cafes full of customers, parks full of promenaders, consulting-rooms of famous doctors full of patients, theaters full of spectators, and beaches full of bathers. What previously was, in general, no problem, now begins to be an everyday one: namely, to find room.

Ortega was ambivalent about all this. No one, he admitted, could begrudge the people more pleasures or better medical

*1992

care. But culture was another matter. He thought that while formerly most travelers were prepared, by training or inheritance, to appreciate art and historic places, the new crowds were not. The latter had come to assert themselves rather than submit themselves; or else—most often, in fact—for no definite purpose. The masses "have decided to advance to the foreground of social life, to occupy the places, to use the instruments, and to enjoy the pleasures hitherto reserved for the few." Though this sounds unexceptionable, "it is evident that these places were never intended for the multitude, for their dimensions are too limited, and the crowd is continuously overflowing them . . ."

I must confess to similar retrograde feelings, especially about tour groups. Swarms of Spanish and Swedish high-school students pinned my companion and me against the wall at the summit of St. Peter's. Everywhere we turned in the Boboli Gardens, we encountered chattering clumps of Italian junior-high-school students. We dashed from room to room in the Pitti Palace, trying to stay ahead of a German group with a very loud guide. The mosaics at Sicily's Piazza Armerina were splendid even in the rain—but only because the many groups present were mostly sheltering in the gift shop and cafeteria. And so on, everywhere.

All this may sound so commonplace, so predictable, so taken-for-granted a travel hazard that there's not much point complaining about it. Actually, I'm not sure, on reflection, that I want to complain. Perhaps the crowd is even a cause for—guarded—celebration, for a muffled cheer. In theory, after all, the cultural landmarks of Europe are everyone's heritage. Better a single confused, brief, distant glimpse of them than yet another generation of ignorance for half the population or more. Many of the crowd will have come for no reason they can articulate; but for others, out of a daily round of routine labor and consumption, the trip may be a shy, wistful homage to the higher life. And even if barren for the traveler, the trip may have a residual effect, may water a seed, blow on a spark, transmit a message to a child, neighbor, or co-worker.

In any case, isn't the increasing activity of the masses—even if painfully inept at first—virtually the definition of political progress? To a democrat and egalitarian, can this publicizing of culture, this subversion of elite privilege, be anything but good? And isn't this large-scale economic and cultural democratization what made possible my own pilgrimage, the child and grandchild of poor, uneducated southern Italian immigrants?

True . . . and yet. Something's not right. It's not a happy match; the places themselves are, in a sense, frustrated. A half-empty theater or sports stadium is a waste; when they're full, both performers and audience are exhilarated. But the Farnese Gardens, the Cappella Palatina, the Greek temples of Sicily can only work their magic on a few visitors at a time. And no doubt they would prefer some visitors to others: erudite old friends and ardent neophytes rather than the dutiful, the acquisitive, the ignorant, or the naively curious.

It doesn't matter, I tell myself; such distinctions are politically invidious, even when made by great monuments (or their imagined spirits). The culturally well-prepared are disproportionately the socio-economically advantaged. Even if it were feasible, as of course it's not, would I really want to penalize the disadvantaged, to compound injustice by restricting their access to "the best places, the relatively refined creations of human culture" (Ortega)?

No, I guess not. Anyway, my purpose here is not to propose a policy, which is a complicated and detailed matter, but merely to sort out my feelings. Am I glad or not that those crowds were there; or better, why am I ambivalent about them? I'm glad that the masses are being made aware of culture. But I'm sorry that this awareness is first awakened through the medium of advertising and therefore perceives culture, at least at first, as an object of consumption. Whether active (i.e., reading their guidebook) or passive, few tourists seemed (I'm speculating, I admit) to recognize that there might be any other qualification for being where they were—in the holy places of European culture—than having paid.

I've quoted Ortega's complaint that the "places hitherto reserved for the few" are now being occupied by "the multitude." Ortega was a Nietzschean conservative and had his own idea of who such places ought to be reserved for:

> The most radical division that it is possible to make of humanity is that which splits it into two classes of creatures: those who make great demands on themselves, piling up difficulties and duties; and those who demand nothing special of themselves, but for whom to live is to be every moment what they already are, without imposing on themselves any effort toward perfection; mere buoys that float on the waves.

Is this a valid distinction? Yes, I believe it is. But Ortega's mistake—what made him a conservative—was his assumption that this distinction between high-quality and low-quality human beings, between creative and critical people on the one hand and passive consumers and conformists on the other, was a metaphysical distinction, a fact of human nature. He never considered that increasing the number of the responsible, the cultivated, and the noble from generation to generation might be possible through a supreme effort of democratic pedagogy. He went, alas, only part of the way with William Morris and Oscar Wilde toward the loftiest conception of socialism yet devised.

If such a pedagogy is undertaken someday—I'm afraid the attempt will not be made in our lifetime, gentle reader, and probably not even in our grandchildren's—there may be just as many visitors on an average day then as now to the great artistic shrines and historic places, or even more. But they won't be crowds.

Publication History

The foregoing pieces were published in the following journals:

AGNI
An Honest Believer
Crowds and Culture

BOOKFORUM
Inwardness
Only Death

BOSTON GLOBE
A Farewell to Virtue

BOSTON PHOENIX
The Shock of the New
Consuming Passions
Disciplines and Bondage
Shipwrecked
The Humanity of Women

BOSTON REVIEW
The Wages of Original Sin

CHRISTIANITY & CRISIS
Solidarity Ever?

DISSENT
Can We Be Good Without God?

HARVARD REVIEW
A Prophet, Honored

NEW HAVEN REVIEW OF BOOKS
Into the Dark?

THE AMERICAN CONSERVATIVE
The Radicalism of Tradition

THE AMERICAN PROSPECT
Growing Pains
Why Be Moral?
Enough . . . for Now

VILLAGE VOICE
A Representative Destiny
The Realm of Freedom
Flatheads of the World, Unite

UNPUBLISHED
Tragedy and Utopia

George Scialabba is a freelance book critic, an editor of *The Baffler*, and the author of *Divided Mind* (2006) and *What Are Intellectuals Good For?* (2009). He lives in Cambridge, Massachusetts, and his work is archived at www.georgescialabba.net.